Change the Picture

A *Xuan Ming Dao* Qigong Workbook

Master Yu-Cheng Huang

Part 1 — Basic Foundations
Includes Levels I & II

Second Edition

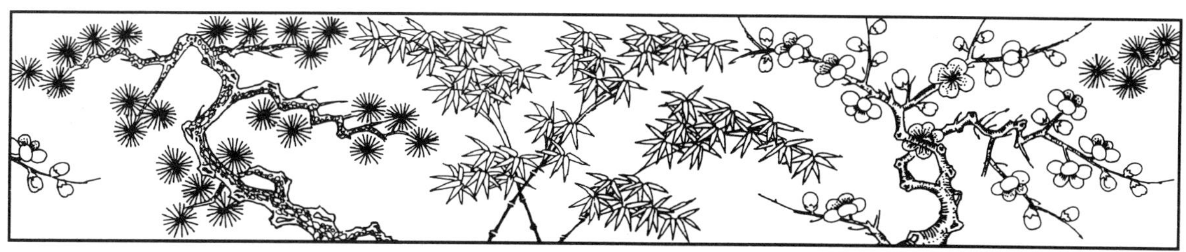

— *Preface* —

I have been practicing Qigong for more than 30 years. When I began practicing Qigong in China it was a turbulent, difficult time in my native land. Qigong sustained and helped me, as it has sustained millions of my countrymen through the centuries. Qigong is not a religion or a way of life, but a means of taking control over the one thing that a person does have a chance of controlling, themselves. You cannot control the times you live in, or the politics of the day, or the economic conditions of your country. But you can find your way in any circumstance if you have the will and determination to know yourself, to change yourself, and to move toward balance. That is what the practice of Qigong is all about.

Qigong is not a mystical science or an easy Far Eastern cure for the stresses, illnesses and problems of modern life. It is a discipline that requires effort and persistence over many years. The very struggle to master Qigong will teach you more about it than any book can.

Some people do not believe that they can really change their lives. I do. If you can make your spirit and energy stronger through the practice of Qigong, you can "change your picture." You can find a "good" picture, and work on a "better" picture. You can begin your journey with this book as your guide.

Our lives are like water flowing to the sea; at times calmly, at times chaotically, sometimes crashing against the rocks, sometimes flowing freely to the sea. We must learn to adjust and keep our own personal internal flow open and smooth no matter what circumstance we encounter. I hope that this book will be a resource that you can use to help yourself and to keep your picture in balance and your body, mind and spirit in harmony. I wish you well on your journey.

Yu-Cheng Huang
at Chicago, July 3, 1996

I wish to thank the following people who assisted in the preparation of this book:

Writing .... Robert Poile, David Cohn, Laurie Manning
Illustration .... Marlene Goodman
Page Layout & Design, 2nd Edition .... George Rumsey
Page Layout & Design, 1st Edition .... Lisa and Tom Jacobsen
Editor .... Laurie Manning
Initial Basic Theory Translation .... Robert Poile, Richard Chan
Photography .... Russ Berkman

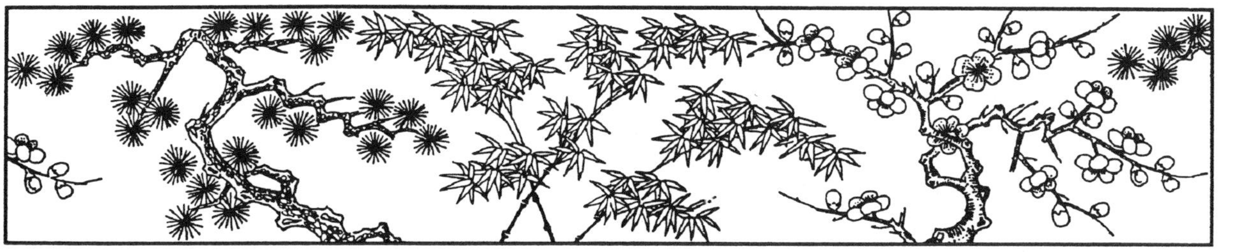

— Table of Contents —

Continued ...

— Introduction —

This book is designed for the beginning student interested in the study of Qigong or the student who is new to *Xuan Ming Dao* Qigong. It provides a progressive program to learn the basic foundation of Qigong. It is intended as a first step. The best approach is to study with a qualified Qigong teacher, however in situations in which this is not possible, this book should assist students in gaining Qigong experience. It is recommended that even if a student is using this book, they should attempt to periodically visit with a teacher in order to insure that their interpretation and application of the practice is correct.

One primary principle of Traditional Chinese Medicine is the necessity for creating and maintaining balance in the body. In this approach to Qigong study emphasis is placed on both theory and method. In each Lesson there is a section on Theory. The Theory in turn deals with one of three aspects of Qigong; areas dealing with theories and principles of Traditional Chinese Medicine (Qigong shares many common principles with TCM); those dealing with principles and theories specific to Qigong; and information on food and its use in dealing with balancing the body.

The section on Method evolves from the Theory and introduces a series of exercises to be completed by the student. The *Xuan Ming Dao* approach to method is integrated. Rather than a single exercise, or a group of exercises, it is a unified whole. Each Level of practice includes a precise pattern of exercises intended to cleanse/prepare, gather, activate and excite the energy, tonify the body and a close which insures all energy is stored in the Dantien. The development and combination of exercises in each Level is based on Chinese theories related to balance including Qi, Yin/Yang, Five Element, Channel Theory, etc. Each Level expands and encompasses the previous Level as the student progresses in the study.

Each person has a different reason for wishing to learn Qigong. Through use of the techniques outlined in this Workbook on a regular basis the individual, over time, can gain many benefits. A few potential results include:

- Keeping the body "open" – this includes the channels, Acupoints, joints, circulation, etc.
- Exciting and activating the body and stimulating the various internal organs and functions. This assists in maintaining an open, free flowing condition in the body.
- Tonifying and strengthening the body and its internal organs, muscles, joints, etc.
- Learning to detect subtle changes in the body which will assist in the monitoring of health and the determination of the body's needs.
- Relaxation and stress reduction.
- Self-treatment, participating in your own health and having some deeper understanding and control over it.
- Learning to self-adjust the body to changes in the internal and external environment.
- Increased longevity, reduced effects of aging, and reversal of old problems.
- Self-maintenance or healing of minor ailments and imbalances.
- Release of muscle tension.
- Stimulation of the energetic system of the body to build vitality.
- Balancing of the body and its energy.
- A deepening spiritual sense and experience.
- Utilization in martial arts.
- Heightened awareness, reaction time, reduction of effect of injuries and strengthening of muscles and bones.

— Using This Workbook —

- It is best to study Qigong with an instructor who you see regularly. Attending classes in *Xuan Ming Dao* Qigong offers a number of opportunities which individual study does not afford. For example:
  - interaction with a qualified Qigong teacher.
  - the instructors assist in activating and opening the points.
  - there is an opportunity to interact with other students and share their questions and experiences.
  - when meditating with a whole group of people, generally there is more good energy generated and received than when a person meditates alone.
  - there are opportunities to practice the methods being used and learn more about their applicability to specific imbalance situations.
  - supervised practice of the utilization of Qi occurs.
  - the energy is adjusted and balanced during the meditation.
  - the student has the opportunity to discuss specific concerns with the instructor and learn whether adjustments are required to make their practice more effective.
  - the instructor can evaluate the manner in which the student is performing the exercises and make corrections as needed.

- Prior to beginning the study the student should consult with their personal physician to insure that this program is appropriate for their situation.

- The student should understand that information contained in this course is a description of Traditional Chinese Medicine, a system of patient treatment based on ancient Chinese philosophy, culture, custom and practice. Master Huang does not intend or represent this course to be medical advice, but simply a description of Traditional Chinese Medicine practices and methods. The student should understand that this course does not qualify any student to self-treat, practice medicine, or give medical advice.

- If the student does not finish a complete Level (i.e. all of Level I or all of Level II), they should not continue to practice the movements being introduced in the study. This is necessary because each Level is balanced within itself as a whole unit. However, each individual exercise may have only one specific aspect. For example some exercises only deal with Yin or Yang energy and practicing them singularly generally would not lead to balance, and might in fact result in the creation of imbalance.

- The student should complete one Lesson per week by reading the theory and then practicing the method for one week before proceeding to the next Lesson. It is important that the study is properly paced in this manner. This allows the energy to develop in a natural, progressive sequence, each Lesson building on the previous one.

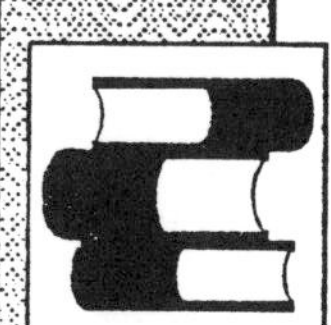

- Each Lesson should be completed as follows:
  - Read the **Theory Lesson**, all Theory Lessons have a "book" symbol by them.
  - Read the **Method Lesson** and practice the new movements individually. After you have practiced the movement individually and feel comfortable with its contents, you should integrate it into the week's practice sequence. All Method Lessons have a "Qi and Buddha" symbol by them.
  - Practice the entire **Practice Sequence**. The Practice Sequence is included in each Lesson and is indicated by the "clock" symbol. It is recommended that the practice be done twice a day if possible, but at least once a day. Good times to practice are between 5 and 7 a.m. and 5 and 7 p.m., times of transition from dark to light when Yin and Yang are in balance. However practice can be done at any time.
  - The **Extra Thought**, (denoted by the "cloud" symbol), **Student Journal** (denoted by the "brush" symbol), and **Student Reactions** sections are optional and can be used in the manner each person feels is most appropriate for their situation.
- Each week the "practice pattern" changes and the student should integrate the new items learned in the proper sequence. Do not change or modify the pattern as outlined. The week's proper sequence pattern is included at the end of each Lesson.
- If the student has any questions, problems, or negative reactions, they should stop practice immediately and consult with a trained Qigong teacher prior to continuing the practice.
- This Workbook covers Level I and II of the *Xuan Ming Dao* Qigong form. Level I and II teach the basic foundation of Qigong practice. In these Levels the goal is to assist students in beginning to become aware of energy, learn to gather energy, and make the energy "stronger." The Stomach and Spleen(digestive system) and Kidneys are strengthened and tonified. Tonification is the therapeutic method that nourishes and invigorates the Qi, blood, fluid, Yin and Yang, organs, etc., of the human body. Whether there is an immediate "sense" of the energy or not, the student most often experiences positive feelings from the practice. Results could include: the student feels stronger; appetite is controlled; sleep is improved; and the individual begins to learn to adjust imbalances.
- A set of audio tapes of the method are available. Please drop us a note at the address below if you would like to purchase the tapes.
- Included at the end of each Lesson is a Student Journal section. It is interesting to annotate your experiences as you progress in the study. I encourage all students to maintain a journal and track their Qigong experience. I am also personally interested in hearing about your experiences and comments. I have included a page for that purpose at the end of this Workbook. You can also send me a note at **P.O. Box 166851, Chicago, IL 60616-6851.**

— A Few Preliminary Cautions —

- These exercises are intended for general health and wellness. They are not designed to treat specific medical problems or concerns. You should consult a physician if you have any concerns about the advisability of beginning this practice, or if you have a specific illness for which you are being treated. Exercises SHOULD NOT be started if you have ANY serious illness unless your physician has been consulted.

- In any of the following cases you should both consult your physician and a qualified Qigong teacher before beginning Qigong practice:
  - If you are pregnant.
  - If suffering with high blood pressure.
  - If you have chronic fatigue syndrome or a similar condition.
  - Any concerns regarding clotting or bleeding.
  - If you have abscesses or blood poisoning.
  - If you are suffering from an acute infectious diseases such as diphtheria, typhoid, measles, chicken pox, etc.
  - If you have a serious illness, such as cancer, hepatitis, tuberculosis, AIDs, etc.
  - Physical impairments (a teacher can help you modify and adapt the exercises to your needs).
  - If you have serious depression, neurosis or psychosis.
  - Questions regarding the appropriateness of practicing during menstruation.

- Avoid becoming tired while performing these exercises. If you become tired, end the practice session by moving in the proper sequence to the close.

- Traditionally it is believed that complete abstinence from sexual activity for a 100 day period at the beginning of Qigong study will help a person find and enhance the energy. In addition, it is best to practice moderation in sexual activities in general.

- The preparations contained in this book are considered primarily as food supplements. Their use is based on ancient Chinese principles and concepts. A person must understand that in the case of any specific problem or illness, their personal physician is the best advisor. It is not intended or recommended that any preparation contained in this book be used to treat any problem without consultation with a qualified professional. Such consultation is absolutely necessary in order to insure that the initial diagnosis of a problem is accurate. After initial diagnosis, imbalance situations must continue to be monitored as methods are applied to correct them. Changes in imbalance situations can be expected to occur either because of remedies used or simply because of other changes (related or unrelated to the initial problem) occurring in the body. Such changes will most often also require modification in approaches to correction.

- Level I, Lesson 2 discusses additional cautions. In addition appropriate precautionary notes are included throughout the study.

Level I

— *Xuan Ming Dao Qigong (Chi Kung)* —
Level I

The name of my method is *Xuan Ming Dao* Qigong. The name has the following meaning:

Cantonese	*syuhn*	旋	*mihng*	明	*dao*	道
Mandarin	*xuan*		*ming*		*tao*	

syuhn/xuan .... A) to roll around B) to return, C) to spin. The circle; circulation; cycles; able to be hard or soft, able to be slow or fast.
mihng/ming .... A) to understand B) bright. Yin/Yang, sun/moon, day/night, understanding.
dao/tao .... the way — path to reward

Level I begins to reveal the way to health and longevity. In the practice, one must pay attention to what happens; ask questions about feelings and experiences. It is also necessary to eat and drink properly, to keep a balanced diet and pay attention to proper nutrition. One learns to eat for proper Qi (chi) balance and to cure poor health.

Lesson 1 呼吸意球功 Method: Breathing — inhalation and exhalation, Part 1
Theory: The generation and control of good energies.

Lesson 2 呼吸意球功 Method: Breathing — inhalation and exhalation, Part 2
Theory: The devil in the fires.

Lesson 3 吸天陽氣 Method: Absorbing the positive forces from the sky (gathering Yang), Part 1
Theory: Preparation for practicing Qigong.

Lesson 4 吸天陽氣 Method: Absorbing the positive forces from the sky (gathering Yang), Part 2
Theory: What to pay attention to during the practice of Qigong.

Lesson 5 採地陰水 Method: Drawing in the earth's negative waters (gathering Yin), Part 1
Theory: Positive reactions and how to conclude the practice of Qigong.

Lesson 6 採地陰水 Method: Drawing in the earth's negative waters (gathering Yin), Part 2
Theory: The relationship between the practice of Qigong and dietary habits.

Lesson 7 心腎相交 Method: Heart and Kidney in harmony (mixing fire and water), Part 1
Theory: Eating and drinking to cure illness and prolong life — Part 1: rice.

Lesson 8 心腎相交 Method: Heart and Kidney in harmony (mixing fire and water), Part 2
Theory: Why practice with an empty or full Stomach is not good.

Lesson 9 天人地合 Method: Bringing heaven, man, and earth together for harmony, Part 1
Theory: Eating and drinking to cure illness and prolong life — Part 2: tea.

Lesson 10 天人地合 Method: Bringing heaven, man, and earth together for harmony, Part 2
Theory: How Qigong promotes health.

Lesson 11 旋明归一 Method: Uniting the earth and sky in the body, Part 1
Theory: Eating and drinking to cure illness and prolong life. Part 3: salt.

Lesson 12 旋明归一 Method: Uniting the earth and sky in the body, Part 2
Theory: Practice schedules — times of day and duration.

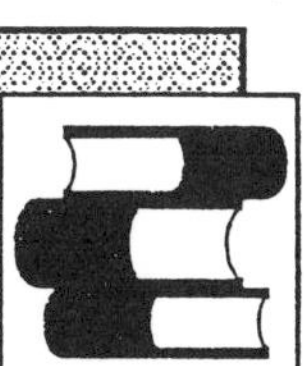

Theory
Level I, Lesson 1

What is Qigong?

Qigong is the study of the energy in the universe. Its focus is on both the internal energy of the body and the energy in the external environment/natural world.

The purpose of the study as taught in this curriculum is to teach energy work — that is learning to identify, control and manipulate energy. The purpose is also to train the student to understand the underlying principles and theories of Qigong. This understanding is absolutely necessary in order to allow the student to develop holistically, and in a progressive, step-by-step balanced manner. To teach the method without the theoretical base would result in disadvantaging the student. The method separated from the theory is both more difficult to understand and more difficult to learn to control and self-apply. As knowledge and ability with Qigong progress, an understanding of theory becomes increasingly important because only by fully understanding the theoretical base can the student begin to properly perceive symptoms and adapt the method as needed to establish and maintain balance/health.

I developed *Xuan Ming Dao* Qigong specifically to provide the best and safest basis for Qigong learning. The curriculum has the following goals:

1. To slowly and systematically train the student to feel and control their internal energy. Qigong also teaches about the energy in the external environment in which the student works and lives. The student progressively learns to utilize energy for wellness, self-healing, longevity, etc.
2. To develop an understanding and ability to apply the underlying theories which govern the practice of Qigong.
3. To insure that each student only proceeds at the appropriate pace in the study, that is the pace which is in consort with their own personal needs and abilities. The Qigong experience will be different for each individual. Some will have an immediate sense of energy, others may not. The important principle to remember is that sensitivity to energy and the establishment of a personal relationship with that energy can be developed through trust in the teacher/method, dedicated practice and patience.

The generation and control of good energies.

Qigong is an ancient art form developed by the Chinese people; it was learned through experience, transforming work to relaxation, sickness to health, and aging to longevity. It is now better understood, recognized and regulated, both in practice and in theory.

The basics, the ABC's, are:

A. The physical stance and practice of the exercise.
   1. structure/posture – performed facing south with the feet parallel, shoulder-width apart, knees slightly bent, weight equally distributed, back straight, head up, chin in — as if suspended by a cord from the top of the head.
   2. relaxation – performed in a relaxed manner, opening yourself and bringing the warmth of the sun's energy into the body.
   3. breathing – breathe naturally, inhaling down to the Dantien area and filling it with the breath.
   4. mental concentration – think of a ball of energy like the sun in the Dantien; focus on its color, its size, its shape, its temperature.
   5. tempo/direction – pay attention to the pulse, the vibration of energy.

B. How Qi circulates in the body to make the organs strong and healthy and how to guide and explore this mysterious force.

C. How to use Qigong to protect the health of the body, prevent sickness, and promote longevity; also for self-curing of illness and strengthening the immune system.

Qigong is part of the Chinese medical tradition, along with herbology, acupuncture, acupressure, massage, etc. It works on the balance of energy in the body organs and channels to maintain a strong, healthy body.

Qigong is of two types — hard and soft; the two types have different applications. Hard Qigong is used for martial arts (iron hand, iron shirt, gold bell, red sand palm) — feats of strength. Soft Qigong is used to keep the body healthy, cure sickness and gain longevity. To learn the hard form of Qigong, one must know and practice the soft form first. Otherwise the practice of the hard form can be detrimental to the health.

Method
Level I, Lesson 1

What preparations should I take before beginning the exercises?

Before Your Practice

- Select a quiet environment if possible.
- Try to pick a time and location where distractions and interruptions will be minimal.
- Wear comfortable clothing and no jewelry, glasses, contacts, etc.
- Empty bowel and bladder prior to beginning exercises.
- Block troublesome and worrisome thoughts from your mind. Try to mentally set aside your exercise time as the time of the day to relax, refresh, and rejuvenate your body.
- Prepare your location to assure comfort. First select a comfortable surface. Then select a comfortable position. If you are practicing lying down, have a mat and pillow, if sitting be certain the chair is ready and comfortable, etc.
- Do not practice when hungry or overly full or right before or after a meal.
- Don't smoke or drink coffee, tea or alcohol before practice. Avoid all other stimulants prior to practice.

During Your Exercise Period

- Learn to concentrate, focus and calm the mind, block vagrant thoughts from the mind.
- Learn to relax.
- Generally the exercises should be practiced in the sequence taught.

After Your Qigong Practice

Try to remember your feelings and experiences with your practice, write in your journal what those reactions are. Over time you will be able to compare and contrast what is happening in your practice.

Always note any 'backfires' or negative experiences and consult with a qualified teacher or Qigong practitioner. The teacher will best be able to determine if adjustments need to be made to practice content and routine. An improper approach to practice can hinder progress in your Qigong study.

Special Points to Remember

- Do not practice when hungry or overly full.
- DO NOT compare your experiences with others, your progress will naturally be different from any other person's because you are a unique individual with a unique background and body composition.
- Generally the exercises are practiced in the sequence taught, however there are exceptions and those are noted as required in the Lessons.

Acupoint Location

Prior to beginning the exercises, it is necessary to know some basic points and areas of the body which are used as part of the practice.

Exercise Objective: To learn to locate the basic points.

	Point	Description
	**Laogong** 劳宫	Found by bending the middle finger tightly inward and touching the palm. Also located at the center of the palm, between the 2nd and 3rd metacarpal bones, but close to the latter. Translated into English this Acupoint means "Palace of Labor." It is located on the Pericardium Channel and is Acupoint PC8.
	**Baihui** 百會	Found by following the ears to the top of the head. A slight indent/soft spot. Can be located on the head, 5 cun directly above the midpoint of the anterior hairline, at the midpoint of the line connecting the apexes of the ears. Translated into English this Acupoint means a "Hundred Meetings" and represents a major Yang meeting point in the head. It is located on the GV or Du Channel of the body and is Acupoint DU20.
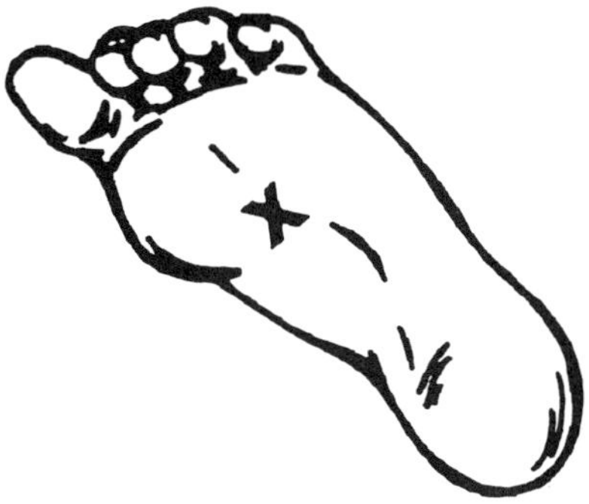	**Yongquan** 湧泉	Found on the bottom of the foot. 1/3 down from the toes or 2/3 up from the heel below the ball of the foot. Can also be defined as located on the sole, in the depression appearing on the anterior part of the sole when the foot is flexed, approximately at the junction of the anterior one-third and posterior two-thirds of the line connecting the base of the 2nd and 3rd toes and the heel. Translated into English this Acupoint means "Bubbling Spring." It is a major Yin Acupoint in the body. It is located on the Kidney Channel of the body and is Acupoint K1.
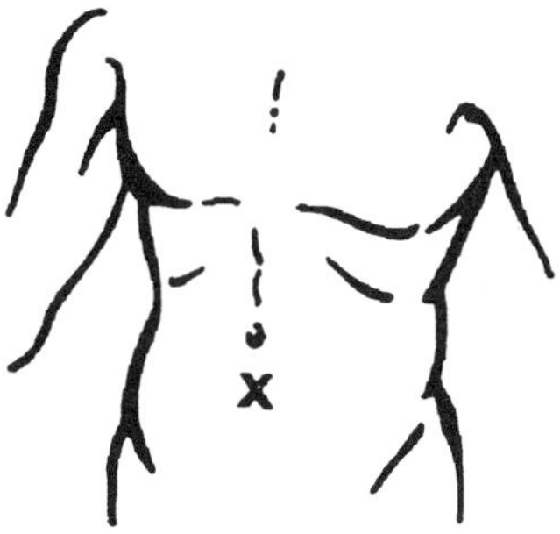	**Dantien** 丹田	Located about three fingers below the navel inside the body between the Bladder and Large Intestine (empty space inside). Translated into English this means "Cinnabar Field." It is considered a major energy storage place in the body. It is not an Acupoint.

The Lesson 1 Method is divided into 4 parts. They are performed in the order listed. Before beginning consider the following:

- Begin facing south with the feet shoulder width apart, parallel and without shoes. We face south to help create balance. The front of the body is Yin, the direction south is Yang; the back of the body is Yang, the direction north is Yin. Thus balance is created. Clothing should be loose, non-restrictive and comfortable. Jewelry and other binding items should not be worn. Breathing is done nasally and preferably from the lower abdomen. With the eyes closed, imagine that the head is supported by a string so that the body is relaxed; the tongue touching the roof of the mouth behind the teeth (by placing the tongue in this position the Ren [CV] Channel which runs down the front of the body, and the Du [GV] Channel which runs down the back of the body are connected); arms are suspended comfortably at the sides; knees slightly bent (not locked); and chin drawn slightly back (without tension). You should smile slightly to relax the body.

Part I — Washing/Cleansing

Exercise Objective: To cleanse the body, mind and internal organs. To prepare the body to begin the exercises. To relax, open points.

Preparation

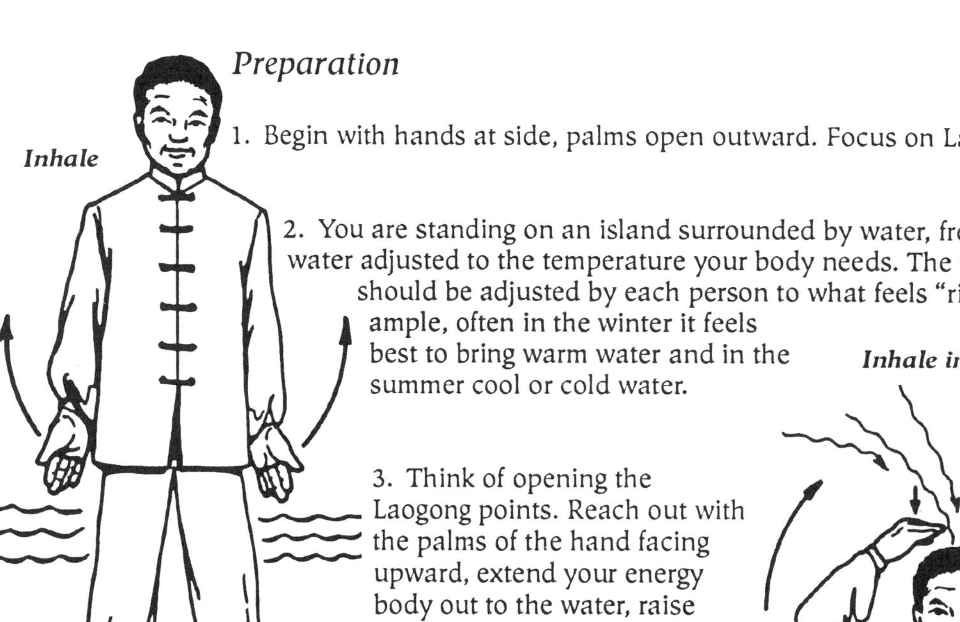

1. Begin with hands at side, palms open outward. Focus on Laogong point.

2. You are standing on an island surrounded by water, fresh, clean, clear water adjusted to the temperature your body needs. The temperature should be adjusted by each person to what feels "right." For example, often in the winter it feels best to bring warm water and in the summer cool or cold water.

3. Think of opening the Laogong points. Reach out with the palms of the hand facing upward, extend your energy body out to the water, raise arms and water to waist level.

4. While inhaling, continue raising the water up until it is over your head.

5. Think of opening the Baihui point. Push the water downward with the hands, palms face downward. Feel the water pouring into the Baihui point. Inhale the entire time you are bringing the water up until the water pours into the Baihui point.

6. As you push the water downward exhale and continue to push down with the two flat hands. If you need to take a breath, pause with the hands while inhaling, and then continue to exhale the water down through the body.

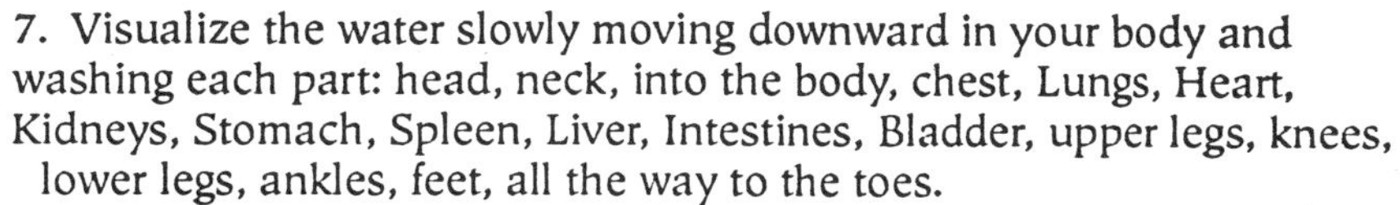

7. Visualize the water slowly moving downward in your body and washing each part: head, neck, into the body, chest, Lungs, Heart, Kidneys, Stomach, Spleen, Liver, Intestines, Bladder, upper legs, knees, lower legs, ankles, feet, all the way to the toes.
   - Notes: 1) As the hands pass the eyes, if the eyes are open, they should close. This will turn the focus inward. 2) When the arms reach the side they hang down in a natural, relaxed manner to the side as the water continues down into the legs to the toes.

Exhale through body

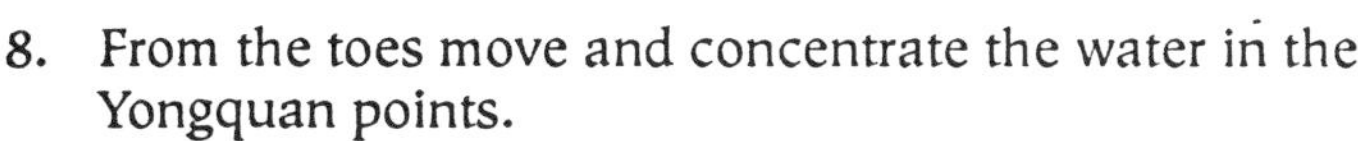

8. From the toes move and concentrate the water in the Yongquan points.

9. Count to 9 while concentrating on the water in the Yongquan.

10. Leave the water in the Yongquan. The concept is that the good energy which is brought in during the remainder of the practice replaces the energy which you have cleansed downward. The "bad" water will naturally dissipate from the Yongquan point. At this time in the study (i.e. the beginning), a student should not try to open the Yongquan to let the energy out, because at the beginning Levels, it is difficult to differentiate the good from the bad energy and good energy might be inadvertently lost.

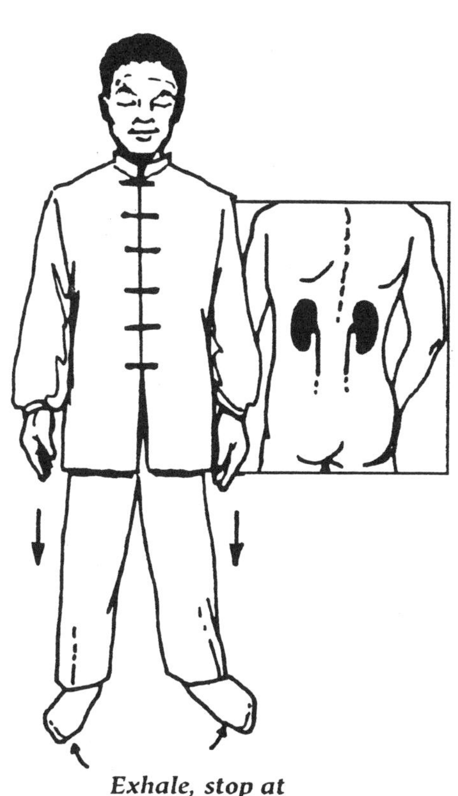

Exhale, stop at Yongquan

11. Repeat the exercise three times.

Part II — Morning sun exercise (Bringing the Morning Sun)

Exercise Objective: To gather the sun or Yang energy as an energy source for the exercises which follow.

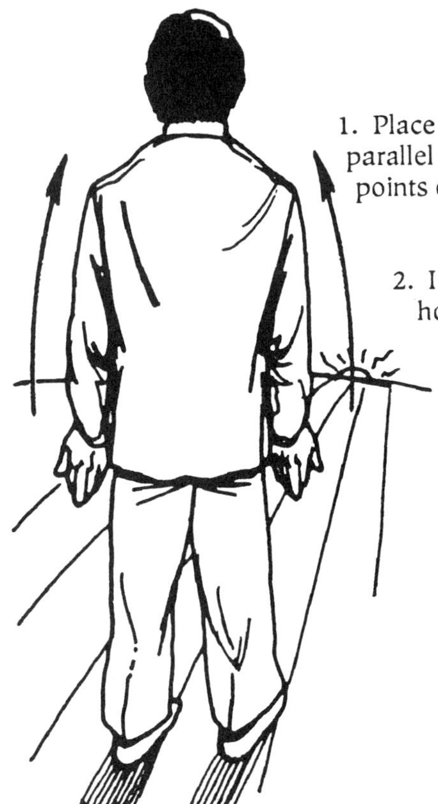

1. Place the hands out in front of body about Dantien height, arms are parallel with the Laogong points turned upward. Think of the Laogong points opening.

2. Imagine a ball of energy, the energy is the morning sun on the horizon. Extend your energy body out to the sun.

3. While inhaling slowly raise the sun up above the head and into the Baihui point (you raise the sun by moving the hands palm upward, up).

4. After sun is in Baihui, form the hands into a triangle, palms pointed forward, fingers pointed upwards, and index fingers touching. Slowly exhale, bring the hands down in front of the body, feel and mentally watch the sun descending down the body's center toward the Dantien. If you need to take a breath, pause with the hands, inhale, then continue to exhale the sun downward to the Dantien.

After sun is in the Baihui, form the triangle.

- Notes: (1) In Qigong in addition to the channels referenced by Traditional Chinese Medicine, there are other channels used specifically for Qigong practice. They are located deeper in the body than the channels used by Acupuncture. When we move the morning sun down through the center of the body we are using one of these special Qigong channels — the Zhongmai or Center Channel. As you advance in your Qigong study, you will learn about other Qigong channels. (2) The hands are kept close to the body as they are moved downward. The hands are an external manifestation of the internal movement of the sun. By keeping the hands close to the body it should assist the student in keeping their focus and the sun moving downward through the center of the body, NOT outside the body.

5. When the Dantien is reached, rotate the hands into an inverted triangle, the thumbs rest on the upper rim of the navel. Fingers pointed down.

6. The sun is mentally placed in the Dantien concentrating the mind there for a short time before beginning the next exercise.

Exhale to Dantien

Part III — Expand and contract the sun

Exercise Objective: To learn to work with the energy; to exchange the internal and external energy; to gather energy and tonify the organs.

....continues from previous exercise

1. Mentally expand the sun from the Dantien outward so that the sun is 2/3 inside the body and 1/3 outside the body. Hands move out in front as this mental expansion is completed. Both hands hold the sun, palms face in toward abdomen at Dantien height.
   - Note: While exhaling think of expanding and radiating the sun through the body and outward. The hands move slightly outward riding the edge of the energy ball. You can think of this as though you were blowing up a balloon.

2. Inhale and contract the sun back to its outside of the body size. That is hands move inward back to 2/3 inside, 1/3 outside position.

3. This exercise is done for at least 5 to 15 minutes.
   - Note: (1) The breathing and the hands move in accordance with each other. (2) The palms are facing inward resting on the edge of the sun's energy at approximately Dantien height. Palms face toward Dantien. (3) Be certain hands face Dantien. If the hands face downward you will drop the ball of energy. If the hands face upward energy may travel to the head. (4) It is important to remember that the energy ball expands outward in all directions. Often because the hands are moving in front of the body the tendancy is to think of the sun moving outward in front. Remember to expand the ball in all directions.

4. After completion, inhale and think of returning all of the energy to the Dantien. Hands rest in inverted triangle over Dantien.

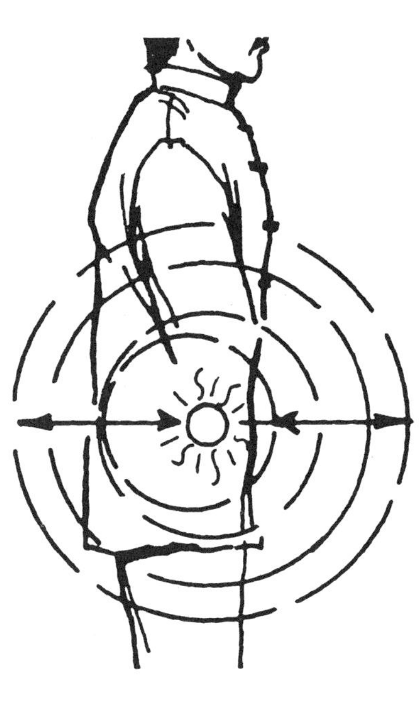

Part IV — Quick close

Exercise objective: To close the energy (simple close)

1. Hands are at Dantien in inverted triangle position. Think about keeping all of the energy in the Dantien.

2. Inhale, think universal energy comes to the whole body, exhale think all energy goes to Dantien. Do inhale/exhale 9 times. The 9 breaths do not have to be consecutive. For example you can take a breath, pause and take a few natural breaths while maintaining concentration on the Dantien, then take the second "concentrated" breath, etc.

3. Insure all energy is sealed in the Dantien.

4. Slowly relax your hands to the side of your body and open your eyes. You should slowly return to action, perhaps massaging the body (i.e. arms and legs), to gently return them to motion. Never rush from the close back into activity, rather allow the body to gradually move back into an active state. Also do not open the eyes too quickly. The eyes are one of the "doors" to energy and if opened too quickly or too wide, energy will escape.

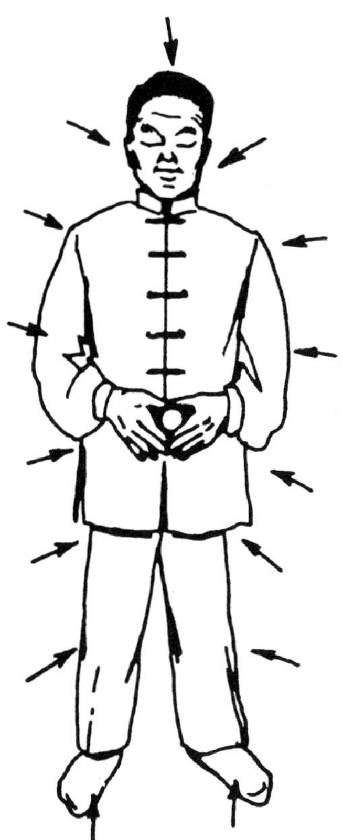

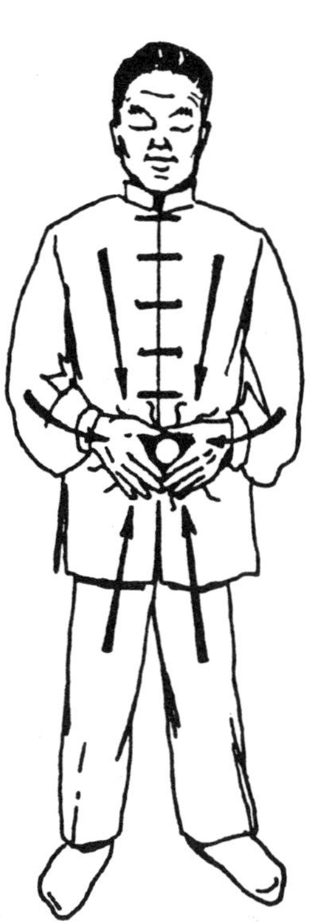

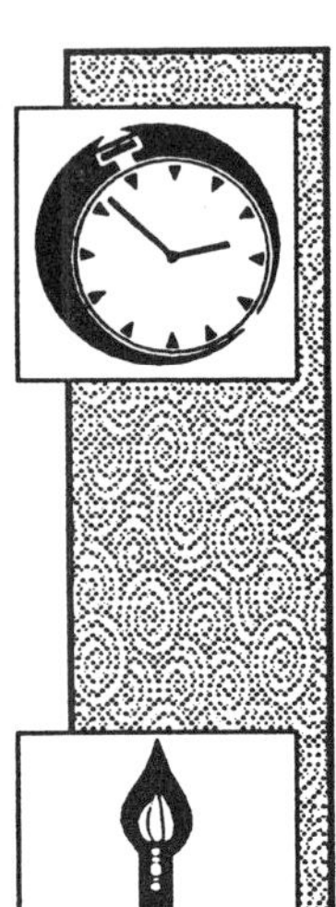

This Week's Sequence of Practice

1. Wash
2. Bring the Morning Sun
3. Expand and Contract the Sun
4. Quick Close

Student Journal

Choose that which is inward, not that which is outward.
— Tao Teh Ching

Extra Thoughts – concentration

Concentration brings focus, force and emphasis to the exercises. If the mind wanders the individual must immediately return the mind to the mental image or body area which is being addressed. Learn to block vagrant, random, and specific thoughts which do not relate to the exercises being performed. Concentration can be improved through dedicated practice and vigilance.

Theory
Level I, Lesson 2

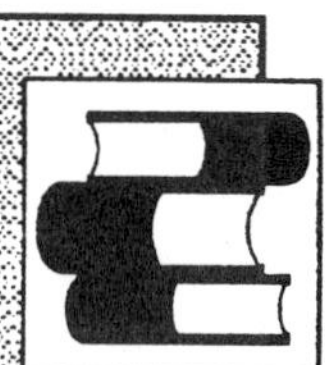

The devil in the fires.

Lesson 2 discusses the causes of 'backfires,' the negative, bad forces, and how they adversely effect the practitioner. It cautions about the effects of bad teaching or incorrect practice, and emphasizes the need to adapt the practice to changes in the body. It stresses that Qigong must be taught individually, since each individual responds personally to the practices.

One might view the practice of Qigong as the climbing of a mountain. When one practices Qigong incorrectly or with an incompetent instructor, it will lead one down the wrong path. A good teacher can take the student step by step to the 'top of the mountain' without wandering off the path.

The main purposes of Qigong practice are to prevent sickness, to develop a stronger body and to promote longevity. Very few people who practice Qigong understand it fully because it is such a large and complex subject matter. One needs to learn to practice balancing the Yin and Yang energies in the body, which change with the seasons and even the time of day. One must understand the response of one's body to the seasons, the predominance of Yin energy in the winter and Yang energy in the summer, and learn to adjust one's practice to the body's changes. To practice correctly, one must first understand each principle and then proceed cautiously.

Some people rush or force their practice. Others practice their own 'way,' thinking to make gains, to produce better, stronger, or earlier results in their practice. The physical symptoms of such variance from the path can be dizziness, headaches, pressure in the head, nausea, nervousness, attacks of panic, and lack of control of bodily movements. In Qigong, these effects are called 'backfires,' or negative energies. These energies can be manifested as both physical and mental symptoms.

If one experiences such ill effects, one must see a Qigong doctor/practitioner to correct them. Only an experienced Qigong practitioner will know how to treat the negative energies. Without treatment, there will be both physical and mental suffering. Therefore, a caution, as stated elsewhere, it is best to practice Qigong under the guidance of a qualified Qigong teacher/practitioner. In addition, it is important to understand that most western medical doctors will not know how to treat the adverse effects of bad practice and how to bring the Yin/Yang forces back into harmony. The student's teacher is the best guide in the case of questions regarding the practice and reactions.

Six causes of backfires, or adverse effects

1. The main reason that backfires occur is that everyone's physical make-up is different and therefore the effects of Qigong practice for each person will be different. As in medicine, certain types and amounts of medicine are needed for certain situations. Thus one must be sensitive to oneself and balance the practice with the seasons and times of day and with their current physical condition.
2. Another reason backfires may occur is changing instructors, or pursuing several different courses of study at the same time. This can disrupt the rhythm of the learning experience. Different teachings can clash and cause ill effects. A person should not practice two forms of energy work at the same time. If however a student chooses to do this, the two practices should be separated, for example practicing one in the morning and the other in the evening. Various specific forms of energy work should NEVER be randomly integrated or combined by the practitioner. Most often alternative approaches have differing methods and principles and the results are certain to be, at a minimum, disruptive to the body and its energy.
3. If not practiced properly, if the instruction is not followed exactly, if one goes one's own way seeking particular results or gains, Qigong can cause bad effects.
4. Misunderstanding the teachings can also cause ill effects. The method of practice must change and adapt to environmental factors such as the seasons and also to the condition of the individual. Practice should never be mechanical, but always adjusted to the situation.
5. If students do not understand the pulse, flow, and circulation of Qi and purposely try to guide the Qi to various parts of the body, adverse effects can occur.
6. Listening to other students' experiences and chasing after them can cause bad reactions. One should listen only to their experienced Qigong teacher in order to be guided properly along the right path. Attempting to duplicate others' experiences can only have ill effects and lead one progressively farther astray.

These six situations lead to 'backfires' and ill effects. However if the student is cautious and follows the correct procedures in their practice, they can avoid the 'devil in the fires.'

Qigong is good for one as long as they practice properly and listen to their instructor. It is not the student or their body which causes the ill effects, but the way Qigong is practiced. It is similar to eating a piece of meat cooked improperly — not enough, too much, in the wrong manner — the incorrect preparation of the meat causes a person to be sick, not the meat itself.

I have placed this precautionary Lesson early in the Qigong study in order to sensitize students to the need for reasoned care in approaching the study of energy. Qi is a powerful force, it's "power" must be respected and treated with caution. Students need to develop and progress sequentially in the practice, constantly evaluating to insure that their understanding, application, and progress is appropriate.

Method
Level I, Lesson 2

Part I — Meditation

Exercise Objective: To tonify, gather energy, self-heal, and store the yang/sun energy.

The sun is in the Dantien from the previous exercise, the hands are in the inverted triangle position. Begin by visualizing the sun's brightness, shape, size, color and temperature. This exercise may be practiced while standing, sitting, or lying, with the spine straight and erect (see section below for more information on practice positions). This part of the exercise is very important and should not be neglected. After the initial visualization and concentration on the sun, the mind may be allowed to free itself, however concentration must be maintained on the Dantien throughout the meditation. I refer to this part of the practice as "watching the movie." The student simply maintains focus on the Dantien and observes the passing scene. Do not allow the mind to focus or concentrate on specific areas of the body or mental images or thoughts during the meditation. If you find this is occurring, always return the visualization to that of the morning sun in the Dantien.

This exercise is done for a longer period than the Expansion and Contraction of Energy (Part III, Lesson 1). That is if you expand and contract the sun for 5 minutes, you should meditate for 10, if you expand and contract the sun for 15 minutes, you should meditate for 20, etc.

- Note: Remember while practicing this exercise that you 'look' inside and try to watch the energy inside the Dantien.

Practice Positions

There are three primary practice positions which can be used during the practice; standing, sitting, and lying down. The position can be changed during the course of the practice. For example the student may wish to begin standing and then later change to a sitting or prone position. This can be done by placing one hand on the Dantien area to guard/hold the energy and then changing positions. After the position is changed, the practice is resumed. Basic principles related to each position are described below. Please note for those who have physical problems which prohibit standing for long periods of time, or at all, ALL methods described can be performed in a sitting or prone position. Some movement modification may be required to accommodate these differences, however provided the thought process is correct and focused, and the breathing proper, beneficial results will be realized from the practice. A teacher can assist in modifying the method.

There are three primary practice positions:

1. Standing

- Hands in inverted triangle at Dantien (thumbs at upper rim of navel)
- Knees slightly bent
- Back is straight
- Relaxed body and mind
- Head up, chin pulled slightly in
- Tongue touching roof of mouth behind the upper teeth
- Smiling slightly

2. Sitting

- If using a chair sit in the front 1/3 of the chair. If sitting on the floor, sit with legs crossed.
- Back is straight
- Relaxed body and mind
- Head up, chin pulled slightly in
- Tongue touching roof of mouth behind the upper teeth
- Smiling slightly
- When meditating and sitting, the hands are not in the inverted triangle, rather they are placed one palm in the other with the thumbs touching.

3. Lying Down

- Lie in a comfortable position
- Have a pillow supporting the head (the head must be higher than the body)
- If necessary place pillows under arms to support them so that hands rest comfortably in inverted triangle at Dantien area (thumbs at upper rim of navel)
- Body lies straight with spine aligned
- Relaxed body and mind
- Tongue touching roof of mouth behind the upper teeth
- Smiling slightly

Part II — Complete close

Exercise Objective: To massage the entire body, "close" and settle the energy, and insure all the energy is stored in the Dantien. In all of the exercises of the complete close, the amount of pressure applied should be adjusted to the comfort level of the individual.

Ia. **Massage of Abdomen** Men place the left palm over the Dantien and the right hand on top of the left with the Laogong points aligned. While inhaling up the left side and exhaling down the right side, move in a circular ever increasing outward spiral. Move the energy inside for 36 revolutions. The first circle should be very small and the last should cover the abdomen. Do not go into the Bladder or rib areas. Breathing, pressure, and timing should be natural and at your own pace. Women should start with the right palm over the Dantien, left hand is on top. Move up the right side while inhaling and down the left side when exhaling.

Ib. **Massage of Abdomen** After completing 36 revolutions stop at the solar-plexus, pause briefly. Men reverse the hands with right palm now on the bottom and the left on top. While going down the left side exhale and when rising up the right side inhale. Women similarly should reverse the hands with the left on the bottom and the right on top while exhaling down the right side and inhaling up the left. The first of these next 36 circles should be large and then reduce the size with each revolution, finally coming to rest over the Dantien. The spiral now moves inward, after 36 revolutions all energy has been returned to the Dantien.

- Notes: (1) In this exercise the student can think of turning the energy outward to collect all energy and then turning the energy inward spiraling it all into the Dantien. (2) If the breathing indicated is not appropriate for your normal rate of breathing, you should adjust your breathing and counting in order to make it relaxed and natural. For example students who breath very slowly may take one inhale for an entire circle, those who breath more quickly may not pay attention to the breathing at all and just count the circles. (3) There are points in the abdomen which correspond to the whole human body. By doing this exercise you are therefore massaging the whole body and all its organs.

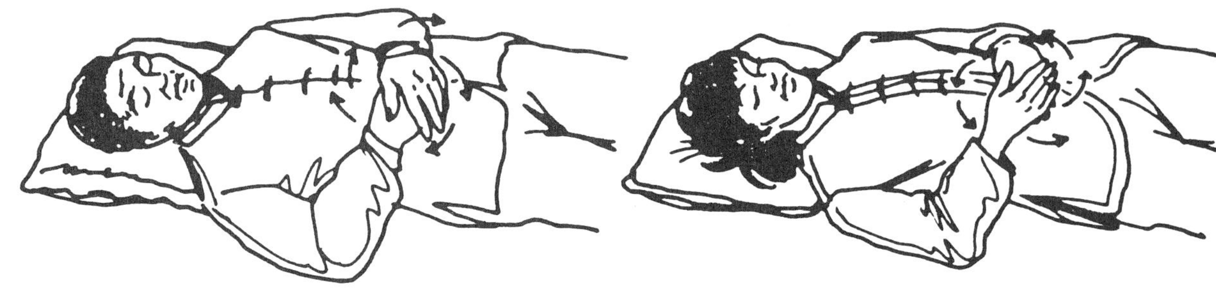

2. **Energy to the Eyes** Briskly rub the hands together to create heat/energy in the palms. Place the palms over the face and eyes. Open the eyes and feel and see the energy radiating into the eyes. Think of inhaling the energy into the eyes, exhale and think of pushing and keeping the energy in the eyes. Inhale energy into eyes 1 to 3 times.

Energy to the eyes

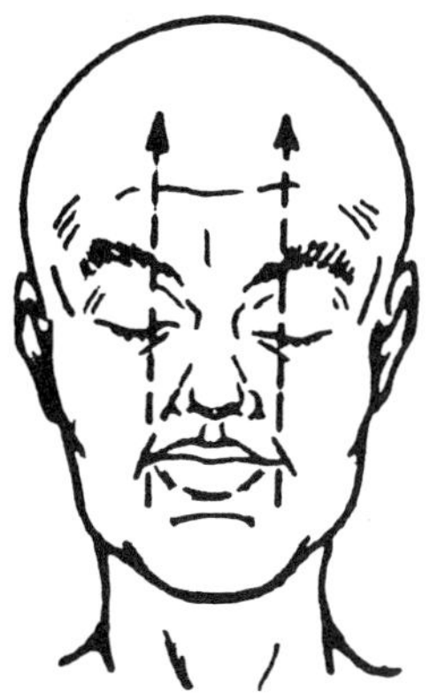

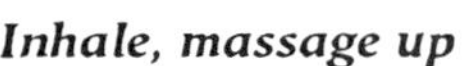

Inhale, massage up

Exhale, massage down

3. **Facial Massage** Rub the palms up the face inhaling, and down the face exhaling. This is repeated nine times making sure that the middle fingers rub the area along the side of the nose and then up into the center of the forehead. The whole palm is flat on the face.

4. **Face Head Neck Massage** Bring the hands to the prayer position. Rub the hands up the face (make sure that the middle fingers rub the area along the side of the nose and then up into the center of the forehead), over the top of the head, down the back of the head, and along the side of the neck beneath the jaw returning to the prayer position. This is done nine times making sure that when the hands rise upward, the breathing is an inhalation and when descending over the top of the head and down, an exhalation.

Inhale up to Baihui. Exhale down back of head.

5. **Ear Massage** The index fingers go to the inner part of each ear with the thumb pressing on the back of the ear. Inhale while bringing the thumb and index finger down the inner part of the ear. Bring the thumb and index finger to the top of the outer part of the ear and exhale while bringing the fingers down to the bottom of the ear to tug on the lobe. Repeat for a total of nine times using a gentle yet firm massage pressure on the ears.
   - Note: There are points on the ear which correspond to the whole human body. By doing this exercise you are therefore massaging the whole body and all its organs.

Inhale inside.

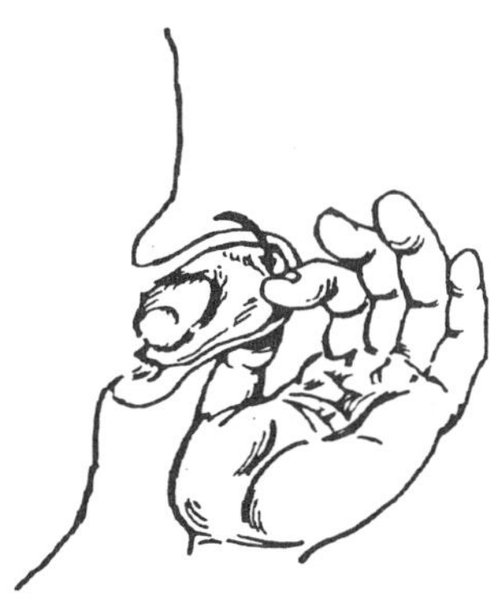

Exhale outer rim.

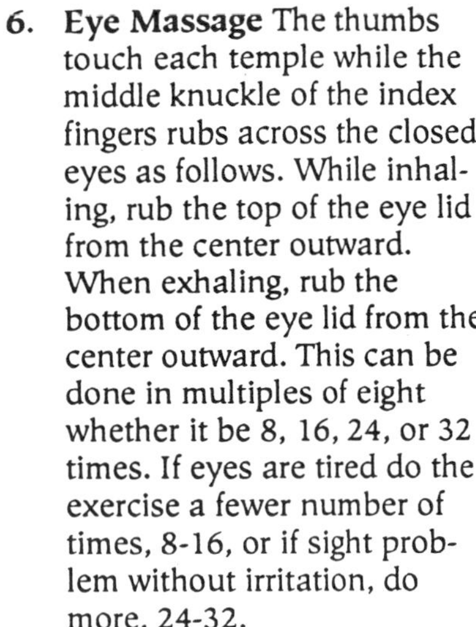

6. **Eye Massage** The thumbs touch each temple while the middle knuckle of the index fingers rubs across the closed eyes as follows. While inhaling, rub the top of the eye lid from the center outward. When exhaling, rub the bottom of the eye lid from the center outward. This can be done in multiples of eight whether it be 8, 16, 24, or 32 times. If eyes are tired do the exercise a fewer number of times, 8-16, or if sight problem without irritation, do more, 24-32.

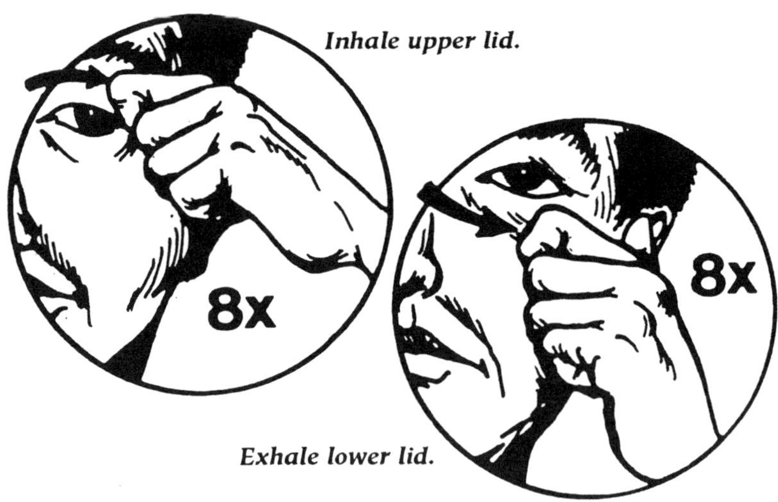

7. **Final** Return to the prayer position, pause for a moment and repeat moving the hands once over the face, top of head, back of the head, neck as before and return to the prayer position. Move the hands downward, when you reach the upper rim of the navel, gently rotate the hands into the inverted triangle position over the Dantien. Pause as long as necessary to be sure that all of the energy has been returned to the Dantien, then slowly open the eyes and relax the hands. This closes the practice session. Slowly return to action.
   - Note: either the full close OR the quick close is done to complete the practice session. The full close is always the preferred choice.

This Week's Sequence of Practice

1. Wash
2. Bring the Morning Sun
3. Expand and Contract the Sun
4. Meditate
   - Note: at this point in the practice, if done at night when going to bed, you may fall asleep and then do the close (quick or complete), the following morning when you arise.
5. Quick or Full Close

Student Journal

Practice non-action and order will occur naturally.
— Tao Teh Ching

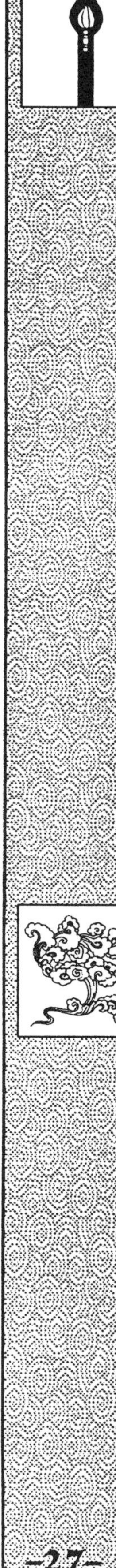

Extra Thoughts – visualization

Specific visualizations during the practice:
In visualization one focuses on seeing an image, for example the morning sun or water. During visualization the effort should not be forced, rather the participant should remain relaxed and continue to consider the visualization. Over time the ability to visualize improves, simply be patient and continue to consider the image even if it does not initially seem clear.

Visualization in meditation:
Visualization in meditation is somewhat different. During the meditation the person begins by considering the morning sun (or the visualization directed by the method) in the Dantien. After this, concentration remains on the Dantien and the mind relaxes and floats freely to undetermined destinations. No single image should be isolated, rather the mind should remain free. The student is an observer, as if they were an objective third party. Further the participant should not try to force a specific image to appear. In addition, once an image is perceived, do not try to continue to hold the image or try to integrate a series of visualizations into some type of story or whole. Rather the mind should simply experience the meditation. If the mind does lose the image or concentration entirely during the meditation and begins to be self-involved, or focuses too long on one thing, always return the mind to the morning sun in the Dantien and begin again.

As an aside it should be noted that some students both see and feel the images associated with the practice very quickly. For others it is a slower process. Some students tend to feel or sense the image rather than see it. Whatever your experience is, you should continue to proceed to try to both visualize and feel the images, accepting that whatever happens in your practice is what is appropriate for you at the time (provided of course the feelings are comfortable). If any images or sensations are experienced which do not feel "right," or are troubling, they should be discussed with a Qigong teacher.

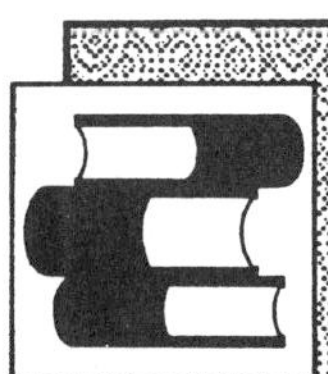

Theory
Level I, Lesson 3

Preparation for practicing Qigong.

With proper preparation one obtains better results. First one must prepare the mind, calming feelings and emotions. Stop both physical and mental activity and concentrate on thinking: *"I am about to practice Qigong."* If a person is extremely upset, they probably should not practice until they are somewhat calm. Practicing when overwrought can actually result in a net loss of energy because the body must use its own energy to try to calm the self and perform the practice. A person can try washing 6 to 9 times. If after that time they are still not calm, they should bring a morning sun, meditate for a few minutes and do the quick close.

Next, pick a quiet atmosphere, indoors or outdoors, such as a park, a forest, most importantly choose a place where not many people or distractions are present. If practicing outdoors it is recommended that the student not stand under a tree, as the energy field of the tree will effect the practice. It is good to practice in the same location every day. This is recommended because, over time, your body creates a relationship with that space which allows you to more quickly reach the meditative state. Regardless of whether indoor or outdoor practice is done, the light should not be too strong and the air should be fresh and clean. Stay out of stagnant or used air and away from pollution. Do not let the wind blow directly on the body, or practice in a draft. Because the points are open it is easy to catch a cold. Keep the body properly warm, not cold; otherwise sickness could occur.

When preparing the practice location have all necessary items such as a chair, pillow, or mat ready prior to beginning the practice. This will insure that the practice does not need to be disrupted once it is in progress. Make the selected area as comfortable as possible before beginning, whether preparing to do lying down, sitting, or standing, Qigong practice. Make sure the location is quiet, so that concentration is not distracted. If interrupted, always close the energy before attending to the distraction. Examples of interruptions might be a knock at the door, the phone ringing, etc. Before addressing the distraction from practice, always return the energy to the Dantien. If for example you must answer the phone during practice, place one hand on the Dantien to hold the energy, then answer the phone. If you are able to quickly say that you will return the call later, you should simply return to the practice. If however you must speak with the person, you should ask the person to wait a moment and do the quick close.

Clothing should be loose and non-restricting. Take off all hard and/or metal objects like rings, watches, belts, glasses, neck chains, earrings, etc. Also take off heavy objects and articles of clothing. Empty bowels and bladder before beginning practice to avoid discomfort or especially interruptions.

Don't practice on either an empty or a full Stomach. One should be neither very hungry nor full when practicing. Do not practice within an hour of a meal. If practicing on waking, take a glass of warm milk or some light warm food before beginning; something must be in the system as a source of Qi/energy. It is preferable that whatever is consumed is warm, this will augment the practice. It is advised that cold and particularly iced or frozen products should not be consumed prior to the practice since these can have a general chilling effect on the body which in turn can effect the ability of the body to generate Yang energy.

Method
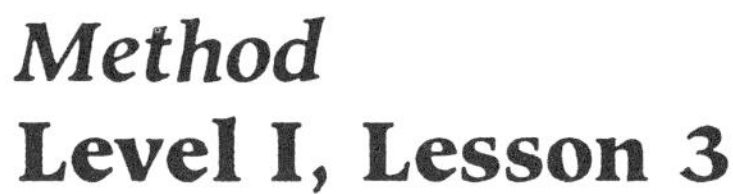

Level I, Lesson 3

Absorbing the positive forces from the sky (gathering yang)

- Note: This exercise is the first of five exercises which are performed in the sequence learned. In each case the exercise is taught the first week. The student spends the first week focusing on the exercise, visualization, etc. The second week the breathing is added. This is done to insure that the first focus is on the physical and energetic movement aspects of the exercise. The breathing is added the second week to assist the movement.

Exercise objective: To gather the Yang energy.

1. Palms turn to back — reach back and up, lean forward and raise up on toes, continue arms up overhead to hold the hot noon sun. Palms turn over to face upward as arm reach out to sides and continue overhead. If you lean backward while moving the arms upward it helps the energy to expand.

2. When arms are straight overhead imagine holding the hot noon sun. Now capture the sun between the palms of the two hands. Palms face each other about 6 - 12 inches apart.

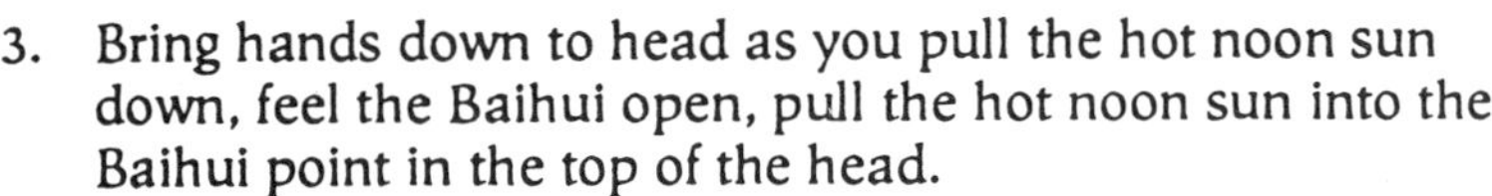

3. Bring hands down to head as you pull the hot noon sun down, feel the Baihui open, pull the hot noon sun into the Baihui point in the top of the head.

- Note: As the hot noon sun is inhaled into the Baihui, return heels to ground.

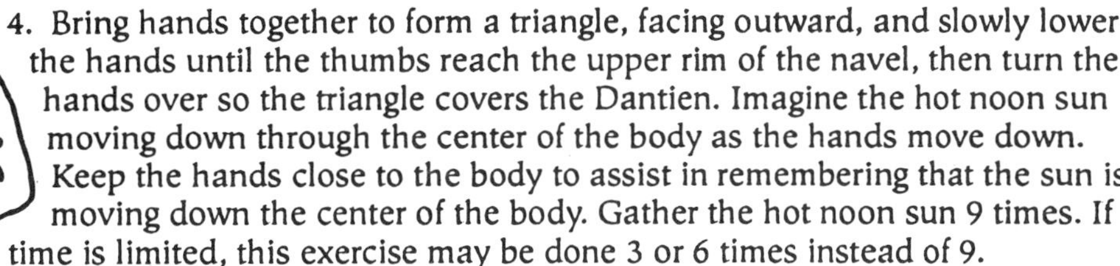

4. Bring hands together to form a triangle, facing outward, and slowly lower the hands until the thumbs reach the upper rim of the navel, then turn the hands over so the triangle covers the Dantien. Imagine the hot noon sun moving down through the center of the body as the hands move down. Keep the hands close to the body to assist in remembering that the sun is moving down the center of the body. Gather the hot noon sun 9 times. If time is limited, this exercise may be done 3 or 6 times instead of 9.

- Note: After the sun has been placed in the Dantien, count to 9 as you watch the sun.

5. Close the Lesson by thinking of the universal energy. Reach out with the palms of the hand, palms upward. Concentrate on the Laogong point. Inhale and bring the arms up, think about gathering new universal energy. Hands come up over Baihui, lower hands palms down, think of pushing all of the energy down and into the Baihui point (all of this is done while still inhaling). While exhaling, think of pushing the energy down through the whole body as you push the hands (flat hand, palm down), downward to the Dantien. When the thumbs reach the upper rim of the navel the hands form the inverted triangle. Concentrate for a few minutes on the energy in the Dantien. This is referred to as the *mini-close* and is done at the end of each of the 5 exercises taught in Level I, Lessons 3-12.

Inhale universal energy into Baihui. Flat hand push energy down to Dantien.

This Week's Sequence of Practice

1. Wash
2. Gather the Yang/Hot Noon Sun
3. Bring the Morning Sun
4. Expand and Contract the Sun
5. Meditate
6. Quick or Full Close

Student Journal

The things which we do not seek to possess absolutely cannot be taken from us.
— Tao Teh Ching

Extra Thoughts – managing change

Managing change is fundamental to our wellbeing and is not an easy task. Just when one becomes comfortable being a child, they find themselves young adults. After adolescence is mastered or at least experienced, a person becomes an adult, job holder, parent, etc. Most often one is expected to be many things at once to many different people. Therefore everyone is in a state of constantly becoming something new and because of this, all are experiencing the challenges and pressures of change. Each person can choose to either struggle against change or learn to accept its inevitability, and adapt to it. If a person does the latter, they can achieve personal harmony; if they cannot, life often becomes an experience of constant frustration.

Qigong does not offer a single or simple answer to dealing with change. Rather it offers an approach or a discipline that helps each person deal with change. Qigong directs its effort toward finding the core of the self, knowing and understanding the flow of energy in the body, and understanding when one is out of balance and how to correct it. Qigong should assist each person in controlling their own personal inner environment so as to readily adapt to the "slings and arrows" of the world around us. The Qigong approach emphasizes a number of imperatives related to personal wellness:

- Philosophically Qigong teaches the student to be prepared to adapt and adjust to maintain personal balance and harmony in whatever situation and area is required. Qigong fosters attentiveness, flexibility, perseverance, and awareness of where oneself and others stand in a given circumstance.
- Qigong provides a series of techniques which can help a person to determine what he or she needs to maintain or re-establish balance, such as cleansing or reducing, strengthening, tonifying, etc. By understanding what is occurring in the body, the student learns to use Qigong, food, and other techniques to insure that they are able to cope with change in the most effective manner.
- Qigong assists the individual in insuring that energy and events flow freely and openly one into another. Qigong tries to facilitate the maintenance of a free flow pattern in the path (Tao) on which each person is moving. By learning to release the self, to view and analyze correctly, to balance as needed, the free internal flow of Qi (energy) is maintained, stagnation prevented, longevity improved.

Managing change requires the regulation of body, mind and spirit. These are all in a state of change so we must regulate them to produce balance. Unregulated the body, mind, and spirit will be haphazard, unrefined and uncoordinated. Regulated they will be in harmony, mature and find their own balance.

We are all in the "*flow of the way.*" Energy flows through and around us, but it can be obstructed, wasted, and diminished. Qigong teaches us how to keep the flow of energy unimpeded, and how to increase, manage, and conserve both the energy and the flow. This kind of control is not achieved in a few Lessons. The arts of meditation, cleansing, and tonifying must be mastered by long practice and instruction. The promise of Qigong, however, is great. It is much more than a coping mechanism. Its purpose is to improve physical and mental health and increase longevity through self awareness, and to invest the individual with the power of self-help and self-healing. Helping us to manage change is one of Qigong's important benefits.

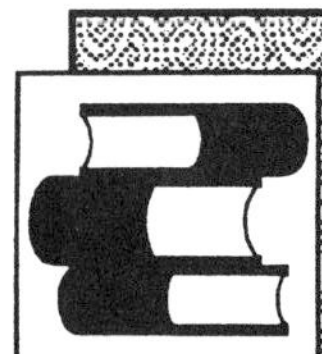

Theory
Level I, Lesson 4

What to pay attention to during the practice of Qigong.

There are many different forms of Qigong, and each of the forms has a different method of practice. However, there are general rules of practice for all forms, they include:

- The posture and position must be comfortable, straight and aligned.
- Each part of the body should be relaxed. Practice with a slight smile, in order to keep the forehead muscles relaxed, an important factor.
- Breathing should be natural and soft exhibiting the five qualities — slow, even, deep, gentle, and smooth. Do not force the breath; control should be natural.
- The thoughts and mental concentration should be light, simple, gentle, not heavy, complex or over-concentrated. Avoid chasing after feelings and thoughts that occur in the mind during practice or trying too hard to recapture previous Qigong experiences.
- Do not panic or become excited. In the event of a loud or sudden noise, keep calm and continue the practice or slowly move to conclude the form.
- Additional advice: difficulty is often experienced in focusing the mind; long practice is necessary. If concentration is lost, one must return the mind's focus to the energy as quickly as possible.

A number of physical effects may be felt during the practice:

1. heat
2. warmth
3. cold (If either too much heat or too little heat is produced, one must adjust the concentration to a middle level.)
4. itching (don't scratch; it's a sign of energy movement)
5. tingling
6. numbness
7. quivering
8. expansion

Keep in mind that in many cases the "line" between a good effect and a problem is narrow. It is based on how you feel. If a sensation is comfortable and feels appropriate, it is most often beneficial. However if it is uncomfortable or disruptive to your practice, it should be discussed with a Qigong teacher.

Method
Level I, Lesson 4

Absorbing the positive forces from the sky (gathering Yang)

Exercise objective: To provide instruction on the appropriate breathing pattern for the exercise learned in Level I, Lesson 3.

Breathing:

1. Inhale as the hands move up to hold the hot noon sun.

Inhale up to sky.

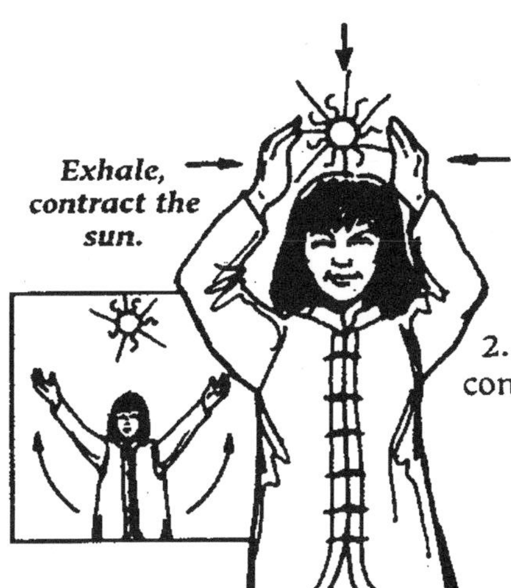

Exhale, contract the sun.

2. Exhale as you capture, contract, concentrate the sun.

3. Inhale as you pull the sun down and in. Hands form inverted triangle facing outward.
4. Exhale as you lower the sun through the body. If you need to pause to take a breath, pause with the hands, inhale, and then continue to exhale the sun to the Dantien.

   - Note: While watching the sun in the Dantien and counting to 9, the breathing is natural.

Inhale sun down and into Baihui.

Exhale sun through center of body to Dantien

5. Exercise is performed 9 times. If time is limited, it may be done 3 or 6 times.
6. Mini-close.

This Week's Sequence of Practice

1. Wash
2. Gather the Yang/Hot Noon Sun
3. Bring the Morning Sun
4. Expand and Contract the Sun
5. Meditate
6. Quick or Full Close

Student Journal

The Tao is limitless and boundless. Though used, it is never depleted.
— Tao Teh Ching

Extra Thoughts – mind control

The mind is one of the most powerful tools available in the quest for wellness. The mind regulates the Qi, blood, bodily fluids and functions of the body. The mind also coordinates the breathing. By learning to utilize and focus the mind, maximum benefits can be obtained from the exercises in this Wordbook. To begin one must relax, achieve quiet, and be as natural as possible. Then the mind can begin to focus (concentrate) itself on the body's energy. These processes should take place without undue exertion. Under the best of circumstances the mind coordinates...

the Qi and blood connected to bodily functions, will, thought, breath, and spirit...
with...
the movements and natural forces...
to...
produce harmony and balance in the body.

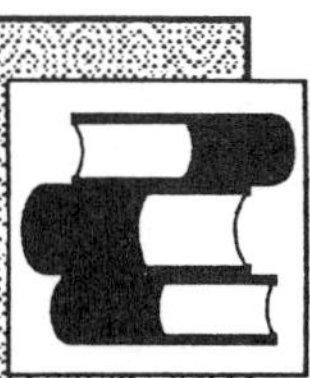

Theory
Level I, Lesson 5

Positive reactions and how to conclude the practice of Qigong.

A person who has good concentration feels and shows a positive reaction to the practice of Qigong. A good reaction for a person who feels sick (loss of appetite, headache, stomachache, etc.) is that they now feel better. If a person has warmth, numbness, tingling, itching, expansion or quivering of the upper body, these are also good signs. The positive mental signs after the practice of Qigong are a clear mind, a feeling of happiness; the body feels fully relaxed, full of energy, and strong — the attitude is positive.

Internally the organs are stronger from being exercised. There will be an increase in appetite, with a person eating more at meals, with digestion and metabolism being more efficient and quicker. The outside physical signs and improvements include:

1. a calmer mind;
2. ease in falling asleep;
3. body weight adjusts slowly up or down as appropriate;
4. the working of the internal organs balance themselves properly;
5. body and mind become more coordinated with quicker reflexes, the person moves more lightly and with more energy, with 'a spring in the step,' not tiredly or heavily.

These are the results of good practice, and thus a check. If these aren't present the practice should be reviewed to insure that all principles and methods are being properly done. The proper practice of Qigong keeps the insides healthy, restores youth, and promotes longevity.

How to finish Qigong practice.

Regardless of whether mental (soft), physical (hard), or a combination of both types of Qigong, are practiced, a proper finish to Qigong practice must be done. Different forms of Qigong have different finishes. One closing is not suitable for all types of practice; the proper rules must be followed to insure that the practice is properly finished or "closed." The proper finish will upgrade the results of Qigong practice. The proper finish will prevent "backfires" from occurring or coming back during the next practice session. A proper finish/closing, as instructed by the teacher, will result in a 'good show.' So far in your study you have learned three closes; the quick close, the full close, and the mini-close. There are many other types of closes which will be learned as the study progresses. Each is intended to insure that energy is stored and controlled.

Method
Level I, Lesson 5

Drawing in the earth's negative waters (gathering Yin)

- Note: here the word "negative" is used in the context of energy being either positive or negative, that is plus, minus, neutral, etc., it does not mean "bad."

Exercise objective: To gather the Yin energy from the earth. This exercise also helps the circulation in the legs and keeps the channels which flow through the legs open and flowing. If stagnation(s) exist in the legs, this exercise can help to reduce or remove the blockage.

1. Place left leg in front (45 degrees/out to side), hands at Dantien. Imagine that you are holding an empty bowl in your hands. The bowl is actually inside the body during this entire exercise. The hand movements are simply an exterior manifestation of the interior energy movement. The physical movement of the hands in this exercise, as in other exercises, is intended to assist the mental imagery. Imagine the leg is empty like a pipe.

2. Move hands holding bowl down to left leg, one hand on each side of leg, palms facing toward leg. Bowl is inside of leg.

3. Move the hands in a circular motion down the left leg moving circles in a clockwise direction. Imagine the bowl is moving and turning through the center of the leg.

4. When you reach the ground continue to mentally circle the bowl into the earth approximately 3 meters (9 feet), to a spring of fresh water. The water's temperature can be adjusted to the temperature which feels most comfortable on this day (e.g. cool in summer, warm in winter).

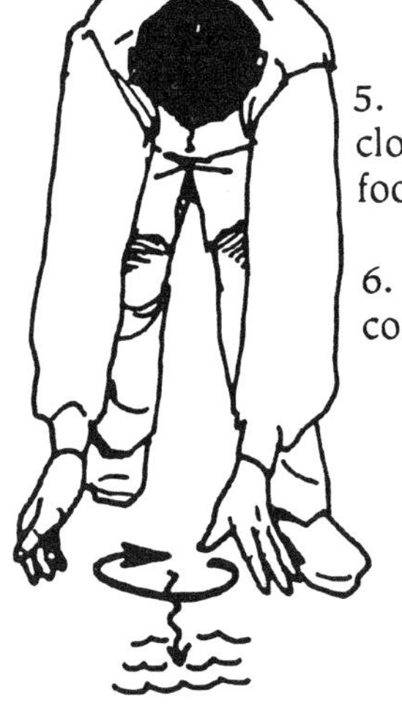

5. Think of scooping water into the bowl. Move hands in circular counter-clockwise direction and bring hands back out of the earth to the foot. Move the bowl through the Yongquan point.

6. Continue moving the bowl filled with water up the leg in counter clockwise circular movements.

7. Return hands to Dantien, pour water into Dantien. Hands are placed in inverted triangle over the Dantien. Concentrate on Dantien as you count to nine.

8. Repeat exercise 6 times on left side.

9. Step back so legs are again shoulder width apart. Then repeat exercise on right leg beginning with number one above (place right leg in front, etc.). Repeat on right side 6 times. If time is limited the exercise may be done 2 or 4 times, instead of 6, on each side.

10. Do the mini-close to finish the Lesson.

This Week's Sequence of Practice

1. Wash
2. Gather the Yang/Hot Noon Sun
3. Gather the Yin/Earth's Negative Waters
4. Bring the Morning Sun
5. Expand and Contract the Sun
6. Meditate
7. Quick or Full Close

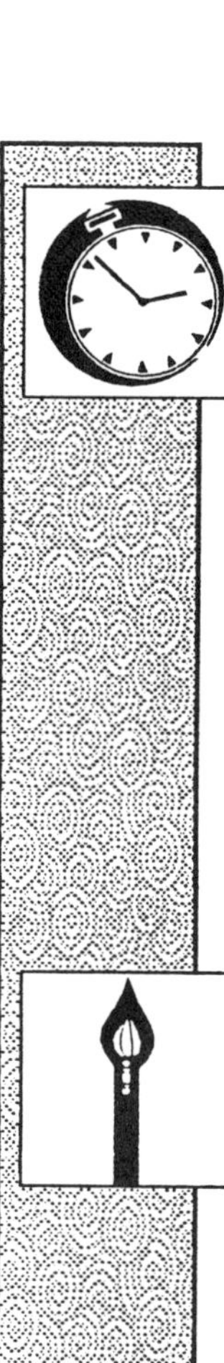

Student Journal

The wise man does his duty, he does not strive to advance beyond others.
— Tao Teh Ching

Extra Thoughts – breathing

Breathing should be natural. It should exhibit the five qualities of slow, even, deep, gentle and smooth. Breathing should be done through the nose and deep into the abdomen. The breathing should be natural and not forced or labored. If breathing does become labored and not natural, the student should pause, consciously relax (place hands on Dantien to hold energy), and continue the practice when breathing returns to normal. Breathing enhances the practice of these exercises and particularly the gathering and directing of Qi.

Natural breathing also enhances the ability to relax by regulating the flow of blood and Qi. Qigong requires that the Qi be smooth and penetrate all the extremities. This is not possible with tense muscles which constrict the blood vessels.

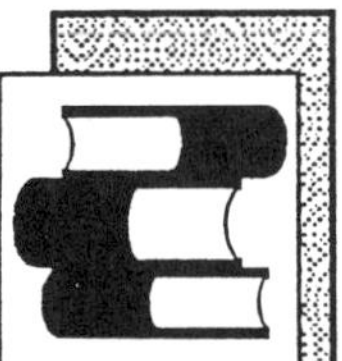

Theory
Level I, Lesson 6

The relationships between the practice of Qigong and dietary habits.

The ancient people suggested that a person should eat an almost vegetarian diet and abstain from smoking and drinking alcohol. They had good reasons for this.

People who eat a balanced diet, sleep, and exercise regularly, have a tendency to live longer and healthier lives. That is why the ancient people recommended that a person eat simply — not heavy and rich food everyday. Consideration must also be given to the fact that the human body needs to absorb the vitamins, minerals, sugars, fat, and proteins from food to subsist. In other words the diet should be balanced and appropriate for the individual person's needs. If a person has a specific health problem and needs to absorb more completely the vitamins from their food, they may need to take in more sugar, protein, and fat. All discussions of specific nutritional needs are of course dependent on the individual condition (e.g. are the teeth in good condition, does the person have any current medical conditions which must be considered such as diabetes, etc.).

Examples of general dietary recommendations include:

1. People with high blood pressure and Heart problems should eat more vegetables and less fat.
2. People with low blood pressure and anemia should eat more minerals, sugars, protein and fat.
3. People with diabetes should consume less sugar.
4. A Qigong practitioner must stop smoking, because cigarettes contain nicotine, a poison — one practices Qigong to dissolve the poisons from the body.
5. A person with arthritis or rheumatism can have a little wine each day, but otherwise, one should abstain from alcohol.

Each person needs to eat to sustain life and health. In addition, food is a primary source of Qi. Therefore daily eating and drinking habits must be examined and modified as needed both to insure good health and proper balance and because they have an effect on Qigong practice. I believe that food can be viewed as the first "medicine." Part of the practice of Qigong is to learn to listen to your body and watch its changes. Through developing this ability we begin to train our "self-doctor." We learn to diagnose ourselves. Because everyone eats each day they are constantly, through the energetic nature of what they eat or do not eat, influencing their body and its functioning. The role of food therefore is critical to any discussion of balance and is an important part of this study.

Many factors go into the selection of foods in cases of maintaining or reestablishing balance. One of them is the Yin or Yang nature of the food. The chart below shows various characteristics that may define a more Yin or Yang condition of the body. Of course there is a balanced state which exists when those two energies are in a proximate state of equality. A person should check themselves the first thing in the morning, before they have eaten anything, and then throughout the day to begin to determine the changes in their condition during the day. If a person has a current problem or is taking medications or preparations, their condition might be affected and the results of the characteristics noted below also affected. In any case of active problems, a trained professional should be consulted to help interpret symptoms and determine root causes. This chart is only intended as the most fundamental and most basic reference to allow the student to begin to gain some experience in sensitizing their analysis of their own body. Once diagnosis is accomplished, then the student can use the tools available to them (such as food, Qigong, etc.) to achieve balance. As you advance in Qigong study, other factors used in determining proper food selection will be discussed.

Yin (-)	Yang (+)
Urine clear & abundant	Urine brief and yellow (concentrated)
Bowel movement soft and loose	Bowel movement hard
Diarrhea	Constipation
Excess saliva	Dry mouth
Feel cold	Feel hot
Listless	Over-active

Many of the recipes or preparations are described using the metric scale. The following conversion table is included for your use:

— Dry Measure —		— Liquid Measure —	
0.035 ounces	1 gram [g]	1 teaspoon	4.9 milliliters [ml]
		1 tablespoon	14.8 milliliters [ml]
1 ounce	28.35 grams [g]	1 cup (8 ounces)	237 milliliters [ml]
		1.06 quarts	1000 milliliters or 1 liter [l]
1 pound	453.59 grams or 0.45 kilograms [kg]	1 fluid ounce	30 milliliters [ml]

Also, when reference is made to a bowl, a bowl is equivalent to 5-6 ounces.

Method
Level I, Lesson 6

Drawing in the earth's negative waters (gathering Yin).

Exercise objective: To provide instruction on the appropriate breathing pattern for the exercise learned in Level I, Lesson 5.

1. Exhale as you move the bowl into the leg and clockwise down into the earth.
2. Inhale as you gather the water into the bowl, and bring the bowl out of the earth and through the Yongquan.
3. Exhale as you move the bowl up the leg counter-clockwise.
4. Inhale as you pour the water into the Dantien.
5. Natural breathing as you count to 9 and watch the water.
6. Close the Lesson by doing the mini-close.

Exhale down the leg.

Continue to exhale into the earth to the water.

Inhale as you scoop the water into the bowl and out of the earth. Continue to inhale into Yongquan. Exhale up to Dantien.

Inhale as you pour water into Dantien.

This Week's Sequence of Practice

1. Wash
2. Gather the Yang/Hot Noon Sun
3. Gather the Yin/Earth's Negative Waters
4. Bring the Morning Sun
5. Expand and Contract the Sun
6. Meditate
7. Quick or Full Close

Student Journal

The wise man does not work for show, he works to complete his task. His desire is not for rewards, but rather for knowing that what he has done, he has done dutifully and well.
— Tao Teh Ching

Extra Thoughts – Yin/Yang

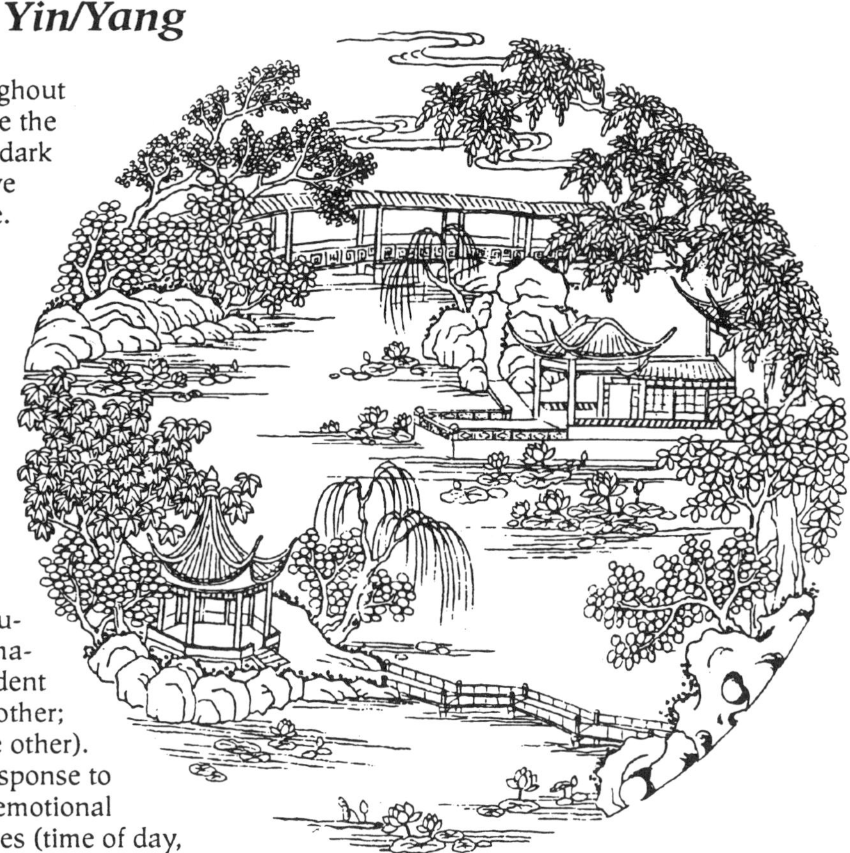

Yin/Yang are terms used throughout Chinese philosophy to describe the two opposite forces in nature, dark and light, hot and cold, positive and negative, male and female. The primary concept behind Chinese medicine is balance, and in discussing balance there are two opposite and conflicting forces that in and through their conflict achieve a balance. In terms of Traditional Chinese Medicine, Yin and Yang are used to describe the competing forces in the body itself, which are constantly seeking balance. The forces are continually in transition and transformation, and mutually interdependent (neither can exist without the other; indeed both are defined by the other). Yin and Yang ebb or flow in response to internal factors (temperature, emotional state, etc.) and to external forces (time of day, season, etc.).

Diagnosis of illness in terms of Yin/Yang theory is most often done in terms of the relative balance or lack of balance of these opposing forces.

The following chart indicates some of the basic characteristics of Yin and Yang.

— Some Basic Characteristics of Yin and Yang —

	— YANG —	— YIN —
Direction	Up/out	Down/in
Time	Day	Night
Season	Spring/Summer	Autumn/Winter
Temperature	Warm/Hot	Cool/Cold
Humidity	Dry	Wet
Weight	Light	Heavy
Light	Bright	Dark
Mood/emotion	Excitable, Hyperactive, Increasing	Quiet, Calm, Decreasing
Other	Male, Sun, Positive	Female, Moon, Negative

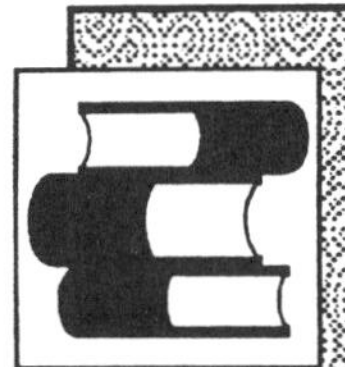

Theory

Level I, Lesson 7

Eating and drinking to cure illness and prolong life – Part 1: rice.

This is the first food Lesson. Food Lesson are generally organized to show some of the following types of information regarding each food discussed:

Energetic Nature of Food .... Yin, Yang, Neutral. Food tastes, as defined by Chinese theory, are also often indicated.

Meridians .... The meridians through which the food "works" are indicated. This means that the food will have the greatest or most immediate effect on the meridians noted. This assists a person in selecting food when trying to use food to balance in general, or to balance in cases where they wish to correct specific imbalances.

Explanation .... Contains general information regarding the food.

Action .... This shows the effect the food has.

Indications .... Shows situations in which the food might be appropriately used.

Contra-indications .... Indicates situations in which the food should not be used.

Preparations .... A variety of preparations are noted. As indicated elsewhere, in cases of specific problems or illnesses, your personal physician should be consulted regarding appropriate treatments.

Rice

Energetic Nature of Food: Rice is neutral. Its taste is slightly sweet.

Action and Meridians: The effect of rice is to balance Yin and Yang and to dissolve the poisons in the system. White rice is neutral and works in the Stomach and Spleen meridians. The best results make Stomach and Spleen healthy, quench thirst, coat the intestines and stop diarrhea.

Explanation: White rice is a primary food substance which also has pharmaceutical properties. The main problems white rice helps cure are upset Stomach (vomiting), excessive urination, constipation, and diarrhea. White rice is a daily food substance for the Chinese people. To use white rice as a health supplement, aged rice is best. Cook the rice as congee (jook – rice soup) to help the Stomach and Spleen grow strong and to clear the Lungs. Congee is suitable for both children and adults and especially those recuperating from weak-Stomach sickness and those who always feel thirsty. The liquid from the rice soup promotes keen eyesight and balances Yin and Yang in the body. It nourishes the five main organs (Liver, Heart, Spleen, Lung, and Kidney). Rice contains vitamins B_1 and B_2, the minerals iron and zinc, and protein.

Ginseng Congee

Recipe for a meal (best in morning and in cool to cold seasons)

- 3g (grams) red ginseng (人参) or 30g 'bastard ginseng' (tang shen 党参) per 100g white rice. Cook the ginseng a long time (overnight for morning use). To make the congee, boil rice for a long time (till the rice breaks apart), and mix the rice and ginseng together. Sugar may be added to taste. Congee may also be prepared by combining the rice and ginseng and cooking overnight in a crock pot. Using this method the amount of ginseng noted above is combined with 8 cups of water and 3/4 cup of rice for a "cereal" consistency congee, or with 10-12 cups of water and 3/4 cup of rice for a more liquid congee (this thinner consistency is the traditional Chinese method of preparation).
  - This recipe will help one's breathing, strengthen the five main organs, quench thirst, and slow aging. It is suitable for elderly people and is a cure for nervousness, shortness of breath, insomnia, poor memory, loss of appetite, anemia, poor sex drive, and continual thirst. It is also good for the Qi and blood. A person with a strong body should eat less congee in the warm-to-hot seasons. After eating red ginseng congee, avoid turnips, bamboo shoots and tea from tea leaves.

Preparations

Note: continue until condition improves or as needed.

1. A cure for diarrhea
   - Heat white rice in a dry pan till dark brown/black, then grind or crush. Take 5g at a time with water, 3 times a day. Continue use until condition improves.

2. Cure for a 'hot' system
   - 100g white rice, 30g ge gen (葛根 Pueraria root) in powder form. Cook the rice as congee (till rice begins to break apart) and add the root powder, stir, and eat. This is good for a 'hot' system which might be indicated by blisters in the mouth, nosebleeds, stomachaches, dry mouth. It quenches thirst and lowers blood pressure. It is good for a weak Heart, Stomach cramps, and age-related diabetes. It is best in spring and summer, but should be taken with caution in fall and winter.

Method
Level I, Lesson 7

Heart and Kidney in harmony (mixing fire and water)

Exercise objective: To gather/mix the Yin and Yang energy. To balance and harmonize the Heart and Kidney. It is noted that in 5 Element theory (one of the primary theories underlying Chinese Medicine), that the Kidney is related to the Heart and is responsible for "controlling" the Heart, that is keeping it in relative balance vis-a-vis the total organ system. This exercise is intended to help maintain the correct balance relationships between these organs.

1. Extend left hand out in front, left foot (45 degree angle) in front, palm up, back knee is bent (weight is on rear leg), left foot rests on heel. Right hand back, palm up. As you stand in this position looking forward, think red, hot/warm, (adjust to what feels comfortable each day), fire, Heart.

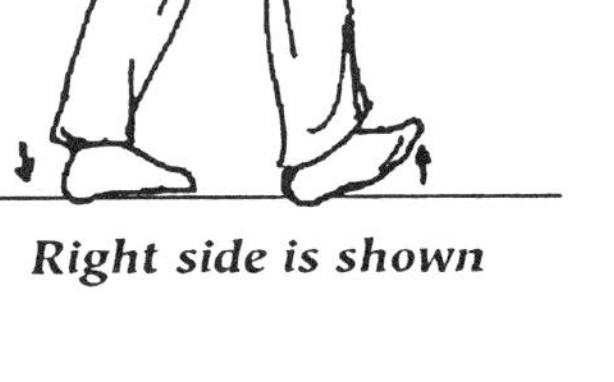

Right side is shown

2. As the hand moves back, turn left hand over so palm is down and move arm down and past side of body to back. When movement is completed left hand faces palm upward in back, body leans forward, head follows hand and looks back, right leg lifts heel. As you look back think black, cold/cool (adjust as needed), water, Kidney.

3. Your opposite hand turns and moves in the opposite direction, i.e. as the left moves back, right moves forward, as in swinging your arms.

4. After 9 times step back with the left foot, place right foot out on heel, right arm should be out in front palm up. Perform exercise on reverse side, same pattern, right hand and foot in front. This exercise is done 9 times on each side. If time is short, exercise may be done 3, or 6 times.

Right side is shown

5. After exercise is performed for last time on second side, return feet to shoulder width apart and relax arms to side. Return all energy to Dantien by doing the mini-close.
   - Notes: (1) Initially if you cannot think of all images associated with the direction at once, choose the one that feels most comfortable that day. For example you might only think red in front and black in back. As time passes and experience is gained, you will be able to think and feel more than one image during a single practice session. (2) Remember that when the arm is in the front your front foot rests on the heel, toe raised and back leg is bent. When arm is at back your front foot is flat and body is leaned forward and the back foot is on toe, heel raised. It is not necessary to think about it because it happens automatically, but when the foot is on the heel or toe the Yongquan point is automatically exposed. This allows creation of another Yin/Yang balance in this exercise. Specifically:

Yin	**Yang**
black	red
cold	hot
water	fire
Kidney	Heart (as compared to Kidney)
north	south
Yongquan	Laogong

This Week's Sequence of Practice

1. Wash
2. Gather the Yang/Hot Noon Sun
3. Gather the Yin/Earth's Negative Waters
4. Heart and Kidney in Harmony
5. Bring the Morning Sun
6. Expand and Contract the Sun
7. Meditate
8. Quick or Full Close

Student Journal

The wise man is aware of what he is, but sets no special store by it.
He respects himself, but does not strive to be ahead of others.
He concentrates on the internal, not the external.
— Tao Teh Ching

Extra Thoughts – quiet

There are three types of quiet: 1) a quiet environment, 2) a physical quiet of the body, 3) a quiet of the mind.

1. **Quiet environment**: When one practices, one must have quiet surroundings; thus one must choose a special place or time to practice. At home for example, this might mean having a room to oneself or waiting until others are asleep.

2. **Physical quiet of the body**: Physical quiet is obtained by eliminating the body's pollutants, e.g., carbon monoxide in the Lungs (quit smoking), digestive wastes (empty bladder and bowels), and muscular aches and tensions (consciously relax the body). Physical quiet starts with stillness. Stillness is achieved when the body is comfortable and motionless. It requires an absence of stress and the release of muscle tension. Therefore when standing we must be balanced not leaning, when sitting we must not lean against something. When lying, our head should be raised slightly.

3. **Quiet of the mind**: Most practitioners of Qigong can attain mental quiet quickly. The method employed is called 'one thought replaces 1,000 thoughts.' This is accomplished by thinking of only one thing — a target, a voice, an image, a single word or phrase, a beautiful happening, etc. Use of this technique, thinking of one thing exclusively, quiets the mind. An experienced practitioner can quiet the mind in an instant. Mental quiet, like physical quiet, seeks stillness. A troubled mind is like turbulent water, the waves obscure the bottom. Turbulent emotions churn up the mind, calm emotions allow for the revelation of the true mind.

Theory
Level I, Lesson 8

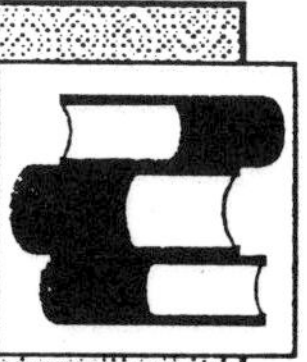

Why practice with an empty or full Stomach is not good.

One purpose of Qigong is to exercise the Stomach and internal organs, thus helping digest food and absorb all the vitamins and minerals from food, producing more energy. Practicing on an empty or full Stomach can have a detrimental effect especially on those with digestive problems.

Practicing on an empty Stomach will activate the Stomach and organs, causing one to feel very hungry and tired. The Dantien, which is located near the Stomach and intestines, is the focal point of practice because the energy causes movement in those regions and turns food into energy. If the Stomach is empty, the practice borrows from one's own energy, and drains one. If one does not eat a little prior to practice, it will disrupt the breathing and rhythm of practice, particularly if one is practicing internally nourishing Qigong.

It is not suitable to practice Qigong right after a meal because the Stomach expands and the Qigong will overwork the Stomach, causing pressure. This will disrupt the breathing and concentration, also causing one to feel uncomfortable. If the Stomach is too full, the practice also drains digestive energy into the Dantien so food will not be digested properly. A person should not practice after drinking alcohol as the Yang of the alcohol will affect the practice.

For best results practice at least one hour before or after a meal. It is best to practice between meals. If one practices in the morning, drink warm milk, some light warm food, or a cup of congee; then practice 20 minutes later. If practicing later in the evening, have something warm and light such as warmed milk before the practice session begins.

Method
Level I, Lesson 8

Heart and Kidney in harmony (mixing fire and water).

Exercise objective: To provide instruction on the appropriate breathing pattern for the exercise learned in Level I, Lesson 7.

Breathing:

1. Inhale on forward movement
2. Exhale on backward movement

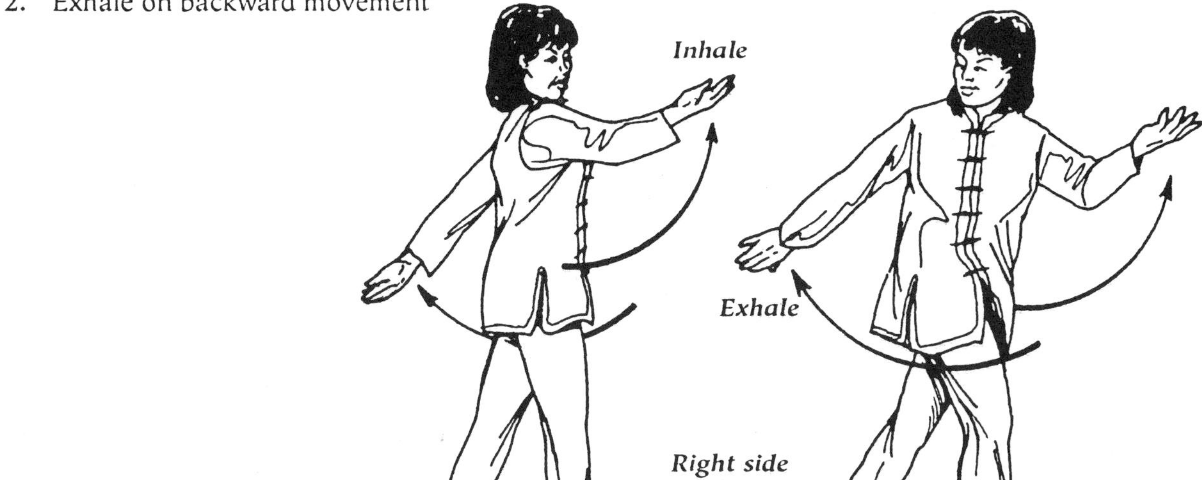

This Week's Sequence of Practice

1. Wash
2. Gather the Yang/Hot Noon Sun
3. Gather the Yin/Earth's Negative Waters
4. Heart and Kidney in Harmony
5. Bring the Morning Sun
6. Expand and Contract the Sun
7. Meditate
8. Quick or Full Close

Student Journal

The wise man understands that knowledge is ignorance. The man who regards ignorance as knowing does not understand the ways of the universe.
— Tao Teh Ching

Extra Thoughts – naturalness

There are four categories included in naturalness:

1. One's surroundings must be natural.
2. One's posture must be natural.
3. One's breathing must be natural.
4. One's thoughts (one's mind and mood) must be natural.

During the practice, everything has to be natural. The goal is for the body, mind and the universe to become one. This cannot be forced, but only achieved with patience, time and practice. How can the body, mind and the universe be described as one? Consider the following situations:

- The weather becomes cool and one doesn't need to add more clothing, or
- It snows in winter and still one doesn't need to bundle up. or
- On a hot summer day, one doesn't need to turn on the air conditioning to be comfortable. or
- One can survive in deep water without drowning or can breathe easily at high altitude.

If one can achieve all of these without any complication, then the person has moved toward becoming one with the universe. This state is not easy to achieve; that is why when we practice, our concentration must be on our posture, our breathing, and the state of our mind, in order to achieve naturalness and move closer to a direct union with the universe.

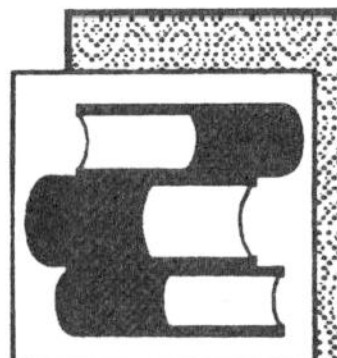

Theory
Level I, Lesson 9

Eating and drinking to cure illness and prolong life – Part 2: leaf tea

Energetic Nature of food: The subject of this Lesson is leaf tea. Green tea has a slightly sweet and bitter taste, is negative or Yin in quality, cold in nature, and has no poisonous effect. It should be noted: Green tea is Yin in nature. Red teas [examples: Lipton, English, etc.], are slightly Yang and increase in Yang the longer they are brewed. Pou lei cha (普洱茶) is balanced or neutral. Herbal teas vary in their Yin/Yang classification based on the energetic nature of the herbs which they contain.

Meridians: Tea works in the system, effecting the Heart, Spleen, Kidney, and Large Intestine meridians.

Action: Tea helps quench thirst, absorbs the grease in the Stomach, raises one's spirits (relieves fatigue), clears internal dampness, and reduces a fever. Tea can help sober a drunk person, aid digestion, assist weight loss, take poison out of one's system, and stop diarrhea.

Indications: Drinking tea is a cure for dry mouth (thirstiness), irregular urination, indigestion, diarrhea, sleepiness, nausea, and obesity. It also absorbs excessive grease from foods, is a general detoxifier, and reduces blood pressure.

Contra-indications: 1) do not drink if taking ginseng or any health tonic; or 2) if having a problem with excessive urination (if urine is clear, Yin); or 3) if experiencing insomnia.

Preparations:
Note: continue until condition improves or as needed.

1. For Stomach cramps:
   - Use 10 small aged (old) red tea leaves and 10g of ginger root mixed or ground together. Start with 2 bowls of water. Simmer together for 30 - 60 minutes to reduce to 1 bowl and form a strong liquid. Drink lukewarm. Discard tea leaves and ginger root.

2. For skin problems:
   - To alleviate skin rashes or boils, use tea leaves to make strong tea and add to bath water or apply directly to clean effected area. This speeds healing and comforts the area.

3. For diarrhea:
   - Mix 1 cup strong green tea with white vinegar (as much as tolerable — up to 40%), and drink.

4. To lower high blood pressure:
   - Mix 3g each of dehydrated chrysanthemum and Huai Hua (槐花) — seeds of a flower — and 3g green tea. Add boiling water to make 1 cup and steep 15 to 30 minutes. Drink 3 - 5 times per day. Discard herb, tea leaves, and chrysanthemum, drink only the liquid.

Method
Level I, Lesson 9

Bringing heaven, man, and earth together for harmony

Exercise objective: To unite "heaven, man and earth," focusing on Yin and Yang energy. This exercise brings in and combines/mixes Yin and Yang energy in the Dantien.

We can imagine that we have a physical body and an energy body. In many of the exercises, including this one, we utilize the energy body to project beyond the limits of our physical body and reach out to interact with and gather either general universal energy or in some cases, specifically Yin or Yang energy. Keep this image in mind, that of an energy body capable of expanding beyond the self, as you do this exercise. I might note as an aside that the energy body includes a spirit body. When we train the energy body we are also training the spirit body. That spirit body is always present although at the beginning Levels, I do not specifically single it out or focus on it. Such a focus and emphasis does however occur in later Levels. At the beginning it is important that the student first focus on learning to feel, control, and strengthen their own energy.

1. For this exercise some students find it more comfortable to place the feet slightly wider apart than shoulder width. Extend arms out to side, palms up. level with shoulders.

2. A) Raise hands over Baihui, B) Press palms up. Imagine that you are extending your energy body up to push the sky and at the same time you are pushing the earth down. You may look upward as you do this.

3. Return hands straight out to side, level with shoulders. As the hands come down you imagine the sky comes down with them. The physical body and energy body are now the same size.

4. Squat down, as you do so imagine that the sky comes down into the Dantien, the earth comes up into the Dantien. Your entire energy body is in the Dantien. It is important in this exercise to maintain the spine in as straight and upright a position as possible. It is better not to go down as low if it causes you to bend forward.
   - Note: The spine is straight to facilitate the free flow of the energy, i.e. energy moves most easily through straight, unobstructed lines.

5. Return to standing position, arms extended, palm up. Physical body and energy body are the same size. Continue moving arms upward and begin second set.

6. This exercise is performed 9 times. If time is limited the number of repetitions may be reduced to 3 or 6. After last repetition return arms to side and feet to shoulder width apart.

7. Close the Lesson by performing the mini-close.
   - Note: This exercise also represents the Chinese concept that man is at the mid-point between heaven and earth.

This Week's Sequence of Practice

1. Wash
2. Gather the Yang/Hot Noon Sun
3. Gather the Yin/Earth's Negative Waters
4. Heart and Kidney in Harmony
5. Bring Heaven, Man and Earth Together for Harmony
6. Bring the Morning Sun
7 Expand and Contract the Sun
8. Meditate
9. Quick or Full Close

Student Journal

When we are tired of being sick, we will be well.
The wise man understands this and therefore is well.
— Tao Teh Ching

Extra Thoughts – relaxation

Three things are necessary to relax completely:

1. the mind and emotions must relax;
2. the joints of the whole body, especially the waist, the neck, and the shoulders, must relax;
3. the internal organs must relax.

To relax means not to be in a stressed or nervous condition; weakness or fatigue will also prevent one from relaxing (since the mind cannot control the body as well when one is fatigued).

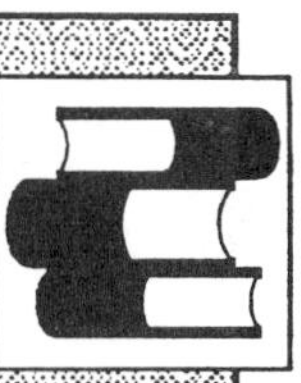

Theory
Level I, Lesson 10

How Qigong promotes health.

The primary reason to practice Qigong is to develop 'special' Qi (also referred to as cultivated Qi). This Qi enhances the normal Qi which everyone has. Qigong study teaches the student to collect and store special Qi in the Dantien. This 'special' Qi strengthens the immune system and can be drawn on in case of illness or injury.

To be fully effective the practice of Qigong has to be relaxed, quiet, natural, and done with a clear (open) mind. This eliminates feelings of stress, anger, and nervousness. It helps smooth the flow of Qi in the channels and causes the blood and Qi to balance in the body. This in turn leads to the organs working in harmony thus avoiding sickness. Qigong practice makes the nervous system more alert, improving reaction time. It helps control brain functions, minimizing worry and therefore aging. It is good for the Stomach and chest, like a massage, increasing appetite, improving metabolism and enabling the digestive system to take in and process more types of food. Regular practice gives a person the ability to use their 'special' Qi to protect themselves against evil influences and bad energy. Qigong practice also increases self-control, and fosters the ability to use Qi to maintain balance/harmony and prevent and rid the self of sickness.

In the practice of Qigong everything is natural — generated from inside the person's own body. Qigong 'medicine' does not need medication or injections to assist in keeping the person healthy and promoting longevity. In Qigong, the Qi works to increase the strength of healthy cells while attacking and ridding the body of the diseased cells, without deleterious side effects.

Method
Level I, Lesson 10

Bringing heaven, man, and earth together for harmony

Exercise objective: To provide instruction on the appropriate breathing pattern for the exercise learned in Level I, Lesson 9.

1. Inhale as the arms move up and over Baihui,
2. Exhale as arms push upward and feet push the earth down,
3. Inhale as arms return to side bringing sky down,
4. Exhale as you squat down and concentrate energy in Dantien.
5. Inhale as you move upward, to begin second set.
6. Close the Lesson by completing the mini-close.

This Week's Sequence of Practice

1. Wash
2. Gather the Yang/Hot Noon Sun
3. Gather the Yin/Earth's Negative Waters
4. Heart and Kidney in Harmony
5. Bring Heaven, Man and Earth Together for Harmony
6. Bring the Morning Sun
7 Expand and Contract the Sun
8. Meditate
9. Quick or Full Close

Student Journal

I have three principles which I hold; compassion, thriftiness and not being afraid not to be first.
Because I have compassion for others, I am able to withstand much.
Thriftiness allows me to be charitable. By not seeking to be first, I can be first.
— Tao Teh Ching

Extra Thoughts – Qi

Qi, in Traditional Chinese Medicine, is the energy which permeates all forms of life in the universe. It is the life force itself. While it may be invisible, it can be felt, controlled, moved, and managed. The quality, quantity, and balance of Qi determines the state of health and longevity.

There are three basic sources of Qi:

- Inherited Qi — obtained from the parents
- Food Qi — derived from food
- Air Qi — acquired from the air

The combination of these three sources is original Qi. Everyone has original Qi.

Qi is what motivates life, movement and change. Qi as the life force and our constant exchange of Qi with the universe, is part of what distinguishes us from inanimate objects.

Level I, Lesson 11

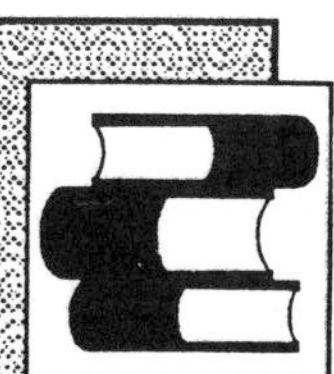

Eating and drinking to cure illness and prolong life – Part 3: salt.

Energetic Nature of Food: The subject of this Lesson is table salt. Salt is one of the basic tastes; it is balanced with respect to Yin/Yang, leaning slightly towards Yin, and it is non-poisonous. The taste is salty.

Meridians: Salt works through the blood system and in the Lung, Stomach, and Kidney meridians.

Explanation: Salt is one of the basic needs of the body along with protein, vitamins, carbohydrates, fat, and water. Salt plays an important part in the digestive system; lack of salt can in fact weaken the digestive system. Salt deficiency causes muscle cramps. Loss of salt through excessive perspiration can cause loss of strength in the hands and feet. Lack of salt for a long period will cause the whole body to weaken and health will fail.

Action: Salt's action helps soften up stiffness, aids bowel movements, and slows vomiting.

Indications: Salt is useful for sore throat, toothache, and congestion (helps loosen phlegm).

Contra-indications: Use salt sparingly if a person is retaining water or has asthma or high blood pressure.

Preparations

Note: continue until condition improves or as needed.

1. For hoarseness, loss of voice:
   - Before singing or public speaking, drink water with a little salt, and hold or gargle in throat.

2. To prevent infection:
   - Apply boiled salty water as a disinfectant to cuts and sores.

3. To prevent hair loss:
   - Long-term use of lightly salted water to wash the hair, especially when followed with a soft-water rinse, conditions hair, adds sheen, and slows hair loss.

4. As an emetic, to promote vomiting in case of poisoning:
   - Heat 1 tbsp of salt in pan till brown; swallow and wash down with warm water.

5. To treat pains in upper back and Stomach:
   - Heat a pound of salt, wrap in cloth, and use heated towel to massage distressed area.

6. For toothache:
   - Brush affected teeth and gums with powdered salt. Also mix salt with Zao Jiao Ci (皂角刺) roast, and use for brushing teeth to strengthen them.

Method
Level I, Lesson 11

Uniting the earth and sky in the body

Exercise objective: Uniting/mixing the Yin and Yang energy in the body. This exercise nourishes the Kidneys.

The Mingmen point is introduced in this exercise.

	Mingmen	
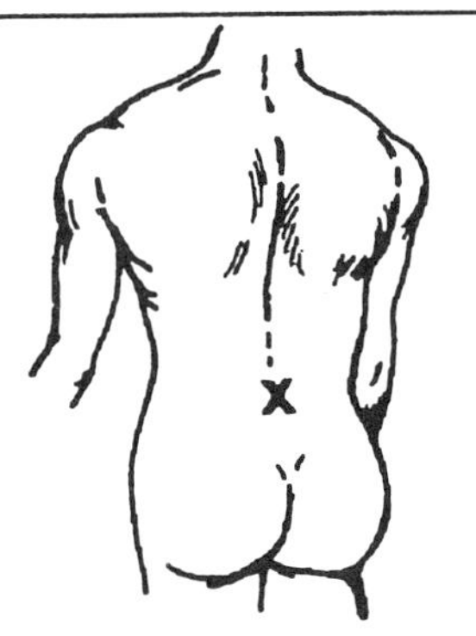	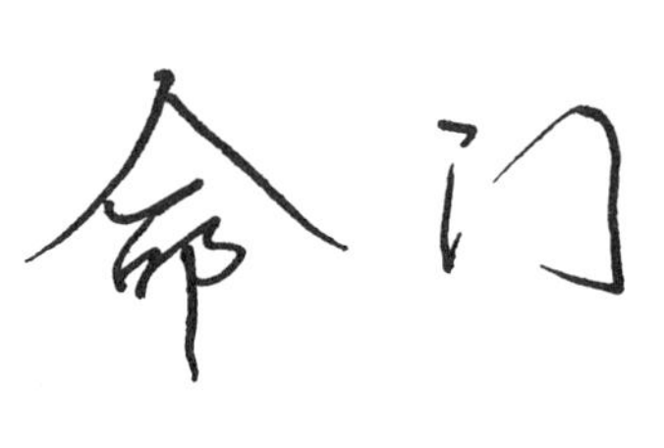	Found by moving directly back from the navel. Also described as located below the spinous process of the 2nd lumbar vertebra. Translated into English this point means "Life's Door or Gate." It is located on the GV/DU Channel of the body and is Acupoint DU 4.

1. Think about Mingmen (life's door).
2. Place both hands to left side (left hand straight out from shoulder, right hand slightly above other arm and pointed left), palms face front. Think of connecting the Laogong points in the hands (about 30% of your concentration) with the Mingmen point (about 70% of your concentration).

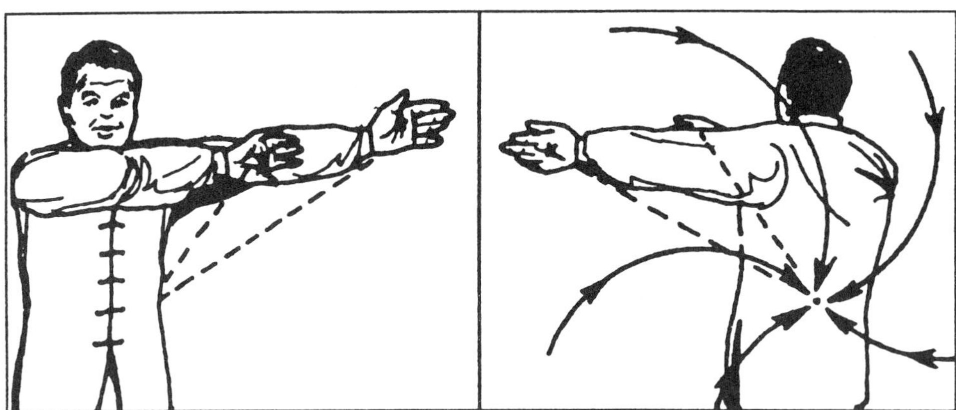

Note: Think of universal energy swirling into Mingmen.

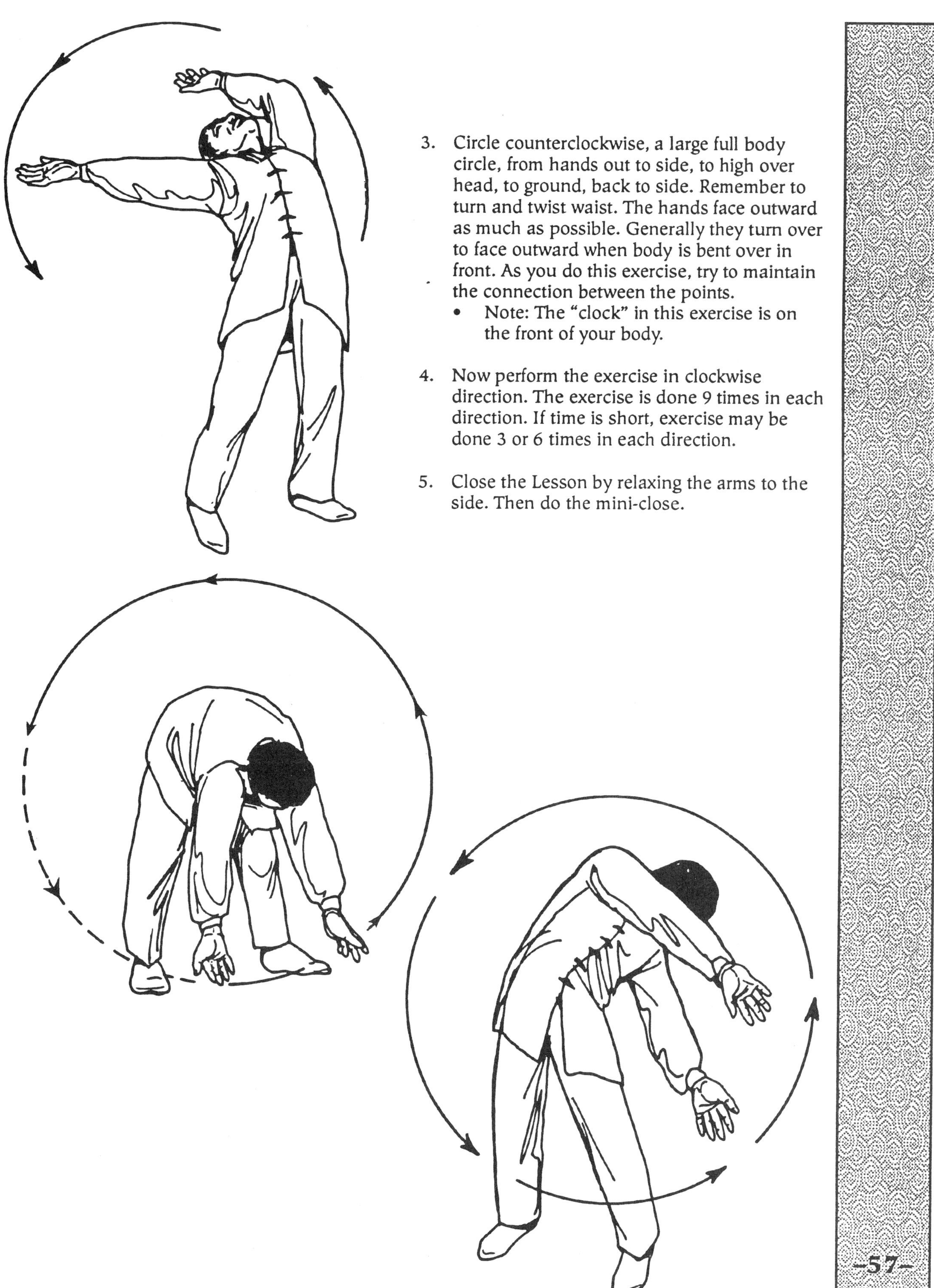

3. Circle counterclockwise, a large full body circle, from hands out to side, to high over head, to ground, back to side. Remember to turn and twist waist. The hands face outward as much as possible. Generally they turn over to face outward when body is bent over in front. As you do this exercise, try to maintain the connection between the points.
    - Note: The "clock" in this exercise is on the front of your body.

4. Now perform the exercise in clockwise direction. The exercise is done 9 times in each direction. If time is short, exercise may be done 3 or 6 times in each direction.

5. Close the Lesson by relaxing the arms to the side. Then do the mini-close.

This Week's Sequence of Practice

1. Wash
2. Gather the Yang/Hot Noon Sun
3. Gather the Yin/Earth's Negative Waters
4. Heart and Kidney in Harmony
5. Bring Heaven, Man and Earth Together for Harmony
6. Unite the Earth and Sky in the Body
7. Bring the Morning Sun
8. Expand and Contract the Sun
9. Meditate
10. Quick or Full Close

Student Journal

Because I do not strive with others, no one can strive with me.
— Tao Teh Ching

Extra Thoughts – basic concepts of TCM

Traditional Chinese Medicine (TCM) developed from a rich background rooted in ancient Chinese philosophy, religion, and science. A few of its basic concepts are:

1. The body is viewed as one whole, a series of balanced, interrelated and interdependent networks and systems.

2. The individual's relationship with the natural world impacts on the internal balance of the human body.

3. A person is "well" when in balance, and "ill" when out of balance. Further, wellness is not just the absence of active symptoms, but a state of well-being.

4. Symptoms do not necessarily identify the root cause of an illness/imbalance. Only by seeking out, identifying and treating root causes can balance be restored.

5. Many illnesses/imbalances are the result of long term processes. Emotional or physical blocks or stagnation are like undiffused time-bombs; when they "go off," they cause acute or chronic problems.

6. The individual person is the prime participant in the control of their health. The person develops into a "self-healer" through the study and use of Traditional Chinese Medicine, and particularly through the study and practice of Qigong. As a "self-healer," the person can reestablish balance and health when treating common imbalances, or in cases of complex imbalances, become a "full partner" with the treating practitioner in restoring balance and health.

7. Food is the first "medicine." Herbs, used as food supplements, are the second.

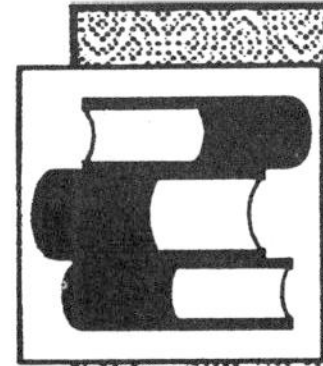

Theory
Level I, Lesson 12

Practice schedules — times of day and duration.

In the practice of Qigong, factors such as the time of day, the length and frequency of practice, etc., depend on the individual. Strong and healthy persons can practice more; weaker and sicker people, less. A young person generally can practice longer than an older one. The practice of Qigong depends on one's bodily condition, and individuals differ, but regardless of condition, all must follow the routine and rules.

Increase practice a little at a time. This means duration and frequency, as well as how vigorously one practices. One may increase practice as long as the practice produces positive results, that is, one's energy is increased and one is content and not fatigued at the end of practice. A beginner who practices and has sore muscles as a result should not worry, this is natural. A severely ill person should not force themselves into arduous practice in order to effect a quick cure, because they will only weaken themselves with 'backfires.'

The best times for Qigong practice are morning and evening, the times of transition from dark to light and light to dark. (These are also the times of proximate balance of Yin [night] and Yang [day] energy in the body). One should begin with 10 to 20 minutes of practice, gradually increasing to 40 and then to 60 minutes, until finally one can practice 2 hours at a time. The frequency of practice can also be increased gradually.

It is best not to practice on either a full or empty Stomach, so one should not wait until just before a meal, when one is very hungry, or just after, when one is full.

Although in general, the more one practices, the better the results, this must be tempered by one's individual characteristics; do not practice to the point of fatigue!

As long as one has determination, correct posture, and follows good instruction, they will achieve the desired results.

Method
Level I, Lesson 12

Uniting the earth and sky in the body

Exercise objective: To provide instruction on the appropriate breathing pattern for the exercise learned in Level I, Lesson 11.

Breathing:

1. Inhale as arms are rising (upper half of circle)
2. Exhale as arms circle down (bottom half of circle)
3. Upon completing last circle, arms relax to side.
4. Close the Lesson by doing the mini-close.

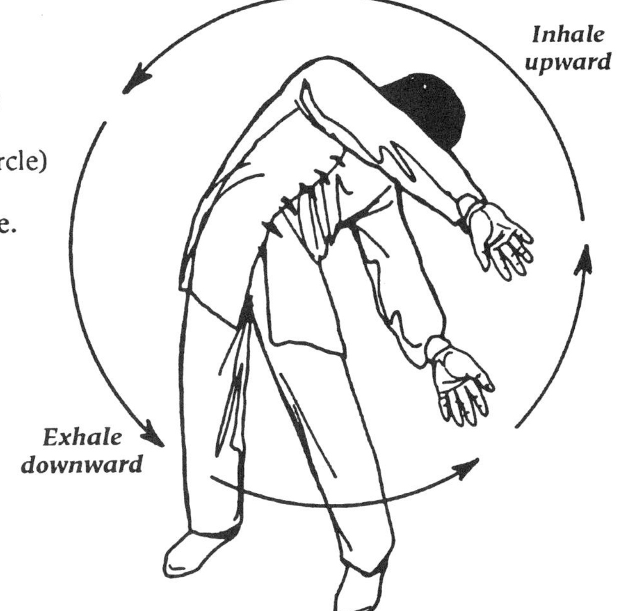

This Week's Sequence of Practice

1. Wash
2. Gather the Yang/Hot Noon Sun
3. Gather the Yin/Earth's Negative Waters
4. Heart and Kidney in Harmony
5. Bring Heaven, Man and Earth Together for Harmony
6. Unite the Earth and Sky in the Body
7. Bring the Morning Sun
8. Expand and Contract the Sun
9. Meditate
10. Quick or Full Close

Student Journal

The wise man helps all to seek and find their own nature by using directionless direction.
— Tao Teh Ching

Extra Thoughts – the body as one whole

Perhaps the primary concept of TCM is the idea that the body must be viewed as an integrated whole. This is the belief that man cannot be separated part from part internally, nor in terms of their relationship with the external environment in which they live.

This concept views man as an integrated whole, that is:

- Organs are interrelated
- Body is connected by meridians, channels, etc.
- Five Element theory defines extended relationships and connectors internally and externally (for example, Liver, associated with wood, spring, eye, green, etc.)

Internal Example: The human body is considered as an organic whole. Within this initial construct special attention is paid to the interrelation and interaction between local pathological changes (that is a change in a single, localized area) and the maladjustment of the body as a whole. Local pathological changes may effect the whole body and pathological changes of the whole body, in turn, may be reflected in a certain part. External diseases may penetrate into the interior and diseases of the organs often have external manifestations. For example:

- Dryness of the eyes is usually due to deficiency of the Liver-Yin, or due to deficiency of the Liver-blood.
- Conjunctival (inflammation of the mucous membrane which lines the inside of the eye) congestion indicates heat in the Liver channel, or excessive heat in the Lung.

External Example: Man and his relationship to the environment:

- Weather—when there are abnormal changes in the natural environment, or when the human body fails to adapt itself to such changes, pathological changes can occur in the body. For example when it is very hot or cold, efforts must be made to balance the effect of those conditions on the body.

It is difficult to make a correct diagnosis of an imbalance situation merely by observing a single or limited number of local symptoms. The body as a whole must be considered as well as its relationship to the external environment.

Level II

— Xuan Ming Dao Qigong —
Level II

Method: The outline of the Method Lessons for Level II is in four parts:

A. The basic fundamentals of Qigong — breath work
B. How the absorption of Qi massages the body
C. How Qigong helps strengthen the Kidneys
D. How to guide the swirl of Qi

Theory: The outline of the Theory Lessons for Level II is in two parts:

A. Qigong and a simple introduction to Chinese medical theory
B. Eating and drinking to cure illness and prolong life.

Lesson 1	筑基功	Method: The basic fundamentals of Qigong - breath work Theory: The existence of Qigong before Chinese medicine.
Lesson 2	筑基功	Method: The basic fundamentals of Qigong - breath work Theory: Eating and drinking to cure illness and prolong life – Part 4: apple.
Lesson 3	筑基功	Method: The basic fundamentals of Qigong - breath work Theory: Where the meaning of Qigong originated.
Lesson 4	浴松功	Method: How the absorption of Qi massages the body/deep wash Theory: Eating and drinking to cure illness and prolong life – Part 5: milk.
Lesson 5	浴松功	Method: How the absorption of Qi massages the body/deep wash Theory: How Qigong was originally introduced.
Lesson 6	浴松功	Method: How the absorption of Qi massages the body /deep wash Theory: Eating and drinking to cure illness and prolong life – Part 6: beef.
Lesson 7	補腎功	Method: How Qigong strengthens the Kidneys Theory: Defining the Qigong doctor and Chinese medical theory.
Lesson 8	補腎功	Method: How Qigong strengthens the Kidneys Theory: Eating and drinking to cure illness and prolong life – Part 7: eggs.
Lesson 9	補腎功	Method: How Qigong strengthens the Kidneys Theory: The formation of Chinese Medical theory
Lesson 10	导旋功	Method: How to guide the swirl of Qi Theory: Eating and drinking to cure illness and prolong life – Part 8: potato.
Lesson 11	导旋功	Method: How to guide the swirl of Qi Theory: The basis of Chinese medical theory and its specialty.
Lesson 12	导旋功	Method: How to guide the swirl of Qi Theory: Eating and drinking to cure illness and prolong life – Part 9: ginger.

Review of Level I

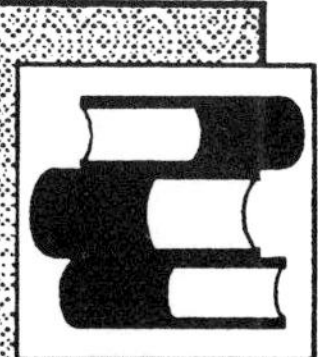

Prior to moving forward, it is appropriate to review the major principles learned in Level I:

- Important factors in preparing for and completing Qigong practice were delineated (time of day, location, stance, diet, length of practice, physical effects, etc.).
- The results of good Qigong practice such as improved attitude, health, sleeping habits, strengthened organs, were noted.
- Possible backfires which can result from incorrect practice were outlined. Any suspected backfires should be discussed with a qualified Qigong instructor.
- The importance of food as a sustainer of life and as the first "medicine" were discussed. Level I began to explore food as a health supplement which can be used alone and in conjunction with herbs to balance the body. Foods studied include:

Food	Yin/Yang	Organ Meridian(s)
Rice	Neutral	Stomach & Spleen
Green Leaf Tea	Yin	Heart, Spleen, Kidney, Large Intestine
Red Leaf Tea	Slightly Yang	
Pou Lei Cha	Neutral	
Salt	Neutral & Slightly Yin	Blood system, Lung, Stomach, Kidney

- The importance of a proper close to the practice was emphasized.

The summary of Level I states:

Level I begins to reveal the way to health and longevity. In the practice, one must pay attention to what happens; ask questions about feelings and experiences. It is also necessary to eat and drink properly, to keep a balanced diet and pay attention to proper nutrition. The student is introduced to the importance of eating for proper Qi balance and to cure poor health.

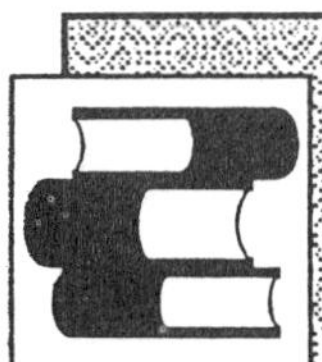

Theory
Level II, Lesson 1

The existence of Qigong before Chinese medicine.

Qigong began more than 5000 years ago in China. At that time people already knew how to use their minds to control internal massage, and how to use "inhalation/exhalation" to cure their bodies' illnesses and promote longevity. Over time these techniques began to be called Qigong.

When some people practiced Qigong, they developed a special ability to see through themselves — their bones, circulatory system, Qi channels/meridians, and acupuncture/pressure points. Also when they ate, they saw the food turn into Qi and travel and collect in different parts of their body to aid in healing and promote wellness. It is from these experiences that Chinese medical theory and herbal medicine began to develop.

Experience and analysis over a long period of time were required to test theories, assemble a unified body of knowledge, and achieve proper results. About 2000 years ago, during the Chinese civil war (Spring/Autumn dynasty), the first Chinese medical book was introduced. It was titled *The Yellow Emperor's Classic on Internal Medicine.* At that time the emperor brought together the best Qigong practitioners in order to gather and analyze their experiences with the use of herbs and various special techniques to effect healing and promote longevity. It was from this point that Chinese medicine began formally developing as a specific body of knowledge. This evolution of Chinese medical theory was prompted by and dependent upon the knowledge and experience base developed by Qigong practitioners.

Method
Review of Level I

Level I is a very important foundation for the study of Qigong. The principles, ideas, and exercises learned at that Level form the basis for proper practice and success in Qigong. In Level I, Qi gathering and movement techniques, were combined with the beginning of visualization, concentration and breath training. All of these areas will continue to be explored, developed and refined in Level II.

You should periodically review the general rules for the practice of Qigong exercises contained at the beginning of Level I.

Examples of Practice Patterns

These examples are offered to show some of the possible manners in which practice can be modified. They should provide a general idea of approaches to making Qigong practice fit within the context of your daily life.

- **Example one: Normal Sequence**
  - The normal or full sequence of practice should be performed on a regular basis. The other examples offered provide acceptable alternatives when time is limited. It is best to practice the entire method twice per day. It is realized that this is not always possible, however students should at a minimum make an effort to do the complete practice at least once a day.

- **Example two: Shortened regular practice**
  - Follow the same sequence as indicated in the first example, however reduce the number of repetitions in multiples of three — that is instead of doing nine repetitions of an exercise, for example do either 6 or 3. These of course should be in proportion to each other. That is if doing 9, you do 9 of all except the Yin exercise which is completed 6 times. If doing 6, you do six of each except the Yin exercise which is done 4 times. If doing 3, you do 3 of each except the Yin exercise which you do 2 times. Always complete the practice by doing either the full close or the quick close.

✱ Example three: Evening meditation immediately prior to going to sleep:

A. In this instance you are doing the full exercise as indicated in example one and then going to sleep:
   1. Complete 3 washes while standing
   2. Perform the exercises while standing
   3. Lie down in bed and then bring the Yang energy/morning sun
   4. Complete the expansion/contraction
   5. Watch the energy (meditate)
   6. Go to sleep
   7. In the morning:
      a. If practicing soon after rising you do not need to close the energy.
      b. If not practicing soon after rising, then do either the full close or the quick close in the morning.

B. In this instance you are just doing Lesson 1 and 2 of the method and then going to sleep:
   1. Lie down in bed,
   2. Complete the three washings
   3. Bring the Yang energy/morning sun
   4. Complete the expansion/contraction
   5. Watch the energy (meditate)
   6. Go to sleep
   7. In the morning:
      a. If practicing soon after rising you do not need to close the energy.
      b. If not practicing soon after rising then do either the full close or the quick close in the morning.

C. In this instance you are going to sleep, but want to do some Qigong prior to sleeping:
   1. Lie down in bed,
   2. Complete the three washings
   3. Bring the Yang energy/morning sun
   4. Watch the energy (meditate)
   5. Go to sleep
   6. In the morning:
      a. If practicing soon after rising you do not need to close the energy.
      b. If not practicing soon after rising then do either the full close or the quick close in the morning.

✱ Example four: Minimum Requirements, modified practice

- In this example time is short and you want to practice, but only want to complete some of the exercises:

A. The practice MUST always include:
   1. Washing
   2. Bringing the Yang morning energy/sun
   3. Meditation
   4. Close (full or quick)

B. In choosing either what exercises to do, if not doing all, or how many repetitions to do, follow these general rules:
   1. Consider whether the exercise is designed to bring Yin or Yang energy. Be certain that the total exercises that you select BALANCE the Yin and Yang energy.
   2. In choosing the number of repetitions of a particular exercise to complete, use multiples of three, six, nine (Yin exercise 2, 4, 6). The exception to this at this level is in the closing, where in doing the eyes, multiples of eight are used.

Notes: (1) In using the above general rules remember, they ARE general rules. Any special cases or needs, should be discussed with a teacher. For examples there may be instances in which a particular condition would require a variance in the practice routine, for example the onset of a cold. However at this level variance must be discussed with a teacher because (to continue our example of a cold), even in the case of a cold the stage of the cold could require the use of a different method (a cold which is just starting, versus a cold that is in the active stage, versus a cold you have had for a month). (2) In Level II three exercises will be taught, plus three separate exercises specifically intended to tonify the Kidney. The Kidney exercises are intended for use in the practice on an "as needed" basis. The other three exercises are part of the regular practice and should be incorporated into your full practice. It is recommended that even when shortening the practice (i.e., fewer exercises or fewer repetitions of exercises), that these three exercises be done at least the minimum number of times.

Method
Level II, Lesson 1

The basic fundamentals of Qigong-breath work

Exercise objective: To tonify organs, train energy. This exercise is also referred to as "moving the sun through the day."

When is exercise performed: During normal Qigong practice, after expand and contract.
✸ Note: This is a three part Lesson taught over this Lesson and the next two.

In this exercise a number of physical and thought changes take place. They are summarized in the chart below:

Time	Hand Position	Temperature	Color	Visualization	Count*
6 am	Dantien	moderate morning sun (increasing)	yellow/orange or as the student visualizes the morning sun	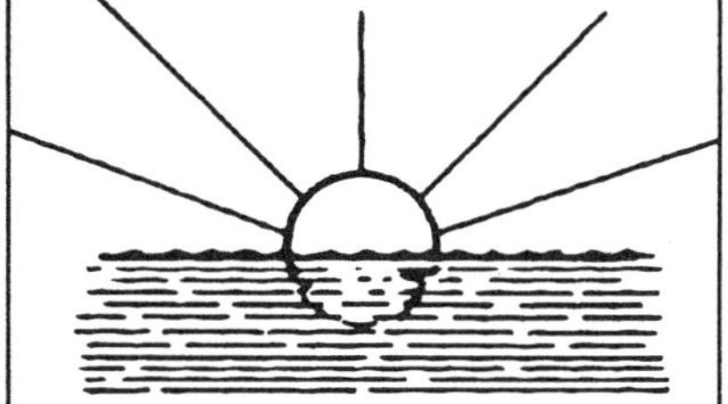	
12 noon	Solar Plexus (thumbs at solar plexus, center of triangle midway between navel & solar plexus)	hot noon sun	bright white/ yellow in color		count to 9
6 pm	Dantien	moderate evening sun (decreasing)	red/orange or as the student visualizes the evening sun		count to 9

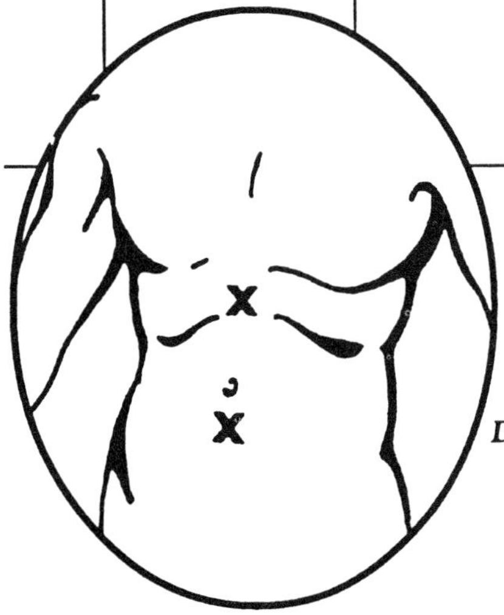

* Note: In Lesson 3 there is also a count of 9 between 6 pm and 6 am.

1. You have just returned the morning sun to the Dantien following the expansion and contraction of the energy exercise. Pause a moment and think of the Dantien. The hands are in an inverted triangle.

2. Change the image in the Dantien of the morning sun to a picture of half sun, half water. The time is 6 am. You see and feel the characteristics noted on the chart on the previous page. The sun occupies the top portion of the Dantien, the water the lower half.

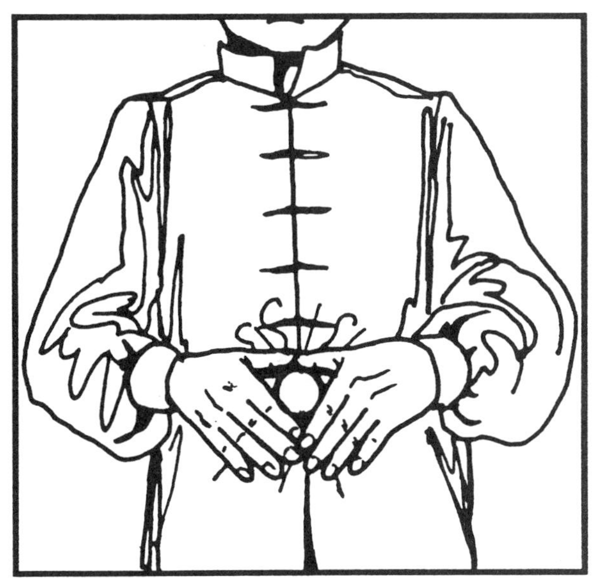

6 a.m. — 1/2 sun, 1/2 water

3. Now move the triangle upward until the thumbs reach the solar plexus. As the sun slowly rises, it changes to a hot noon sun. When the thumbs reach the solar plexus the hands are in the triangle pointed downward. Visualize and feel the hot noon sun. Count to 9. Inhale as the hands move upward.

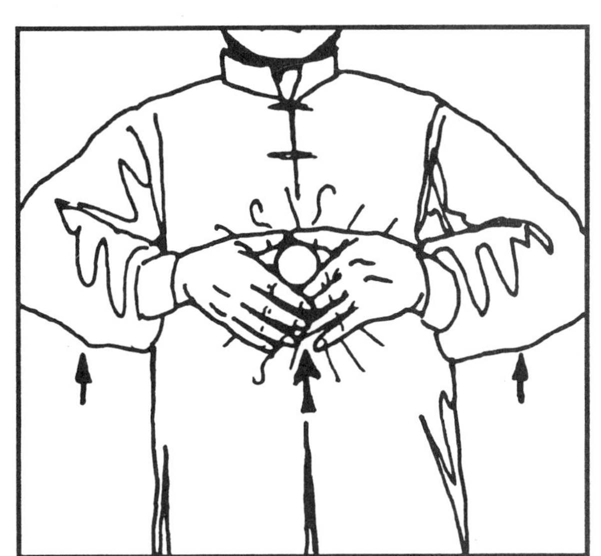

12 noon — hot noon sun

4. Return triangle downward to Dantien. As you move downward the time changes from 12 noon to 6pm. You see and feel the evening sun/water visualizations. Exhale as you move the hands downward. As you count to 9, mentally move from the 6 pm visualization to the 6 am visualization. The hands do not change position, but the picture changes.

5. Repeat this exercise 9-36 times.

6. After completion begin the meditation on the visualization of the 6 am half sun, half water image in the Dantien.

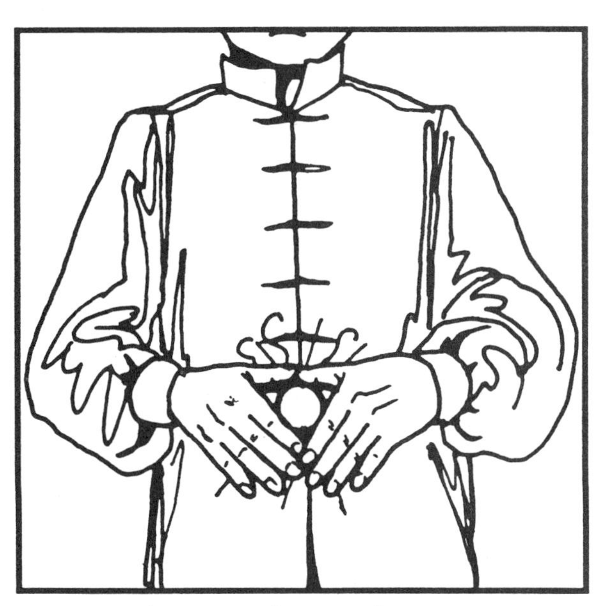

6 p.m. — 1/2 sun, 1/2 water

This Week's Sequence of Practice

1. Wash
2. Gather the Yang/Hot Noon Sun
3. Gather the Yin/Earth's Negative Waters
4. Heart and Kidney in Harmony
5. Bring Heaven, Man and Earth Together for Harmony
6. Unite the Earth and Sky in the Body
7. Bring the Morning Sun
8. Expand and Contract the Sun
9. Move the Sun Through the Day
10. Meditate
11. Quick or Full Close

Student Journal

He who knows does not speak.
He who speaks does not know.
— Tao Teh Ching

Extra Thoughts – the importance of prevention

Qigong allows a practitioner to recognize and treat imbalances before they appear as serious or active symptoms. The development of the ability to protect the body by maintaining balance and preventing imbalance from occurring is a critical goal of Qigong. The ancients said:

> *...the Sages did not treat the sick, they treated those who were not yet sick; they did not regulate chaos, they introduced regulations prior to the emergence of chaos. That is meant here. Hence, if medications are applied only after a disease has become manifest, or if regulations are introduced only after chaos has emerged, is that not equally late as the digging of wells when one is thirsty, or the forging of weapons in the event of war?*

Ongoing regulation and balancing in TCM is done through practices such as Qigong, diet, acupressure, acupuncture, massage, etc.

TCM's approach relies as much on preventative as curative techniques. It also manages recovery and recuperative processes well because it recognizes different stages and types of specific conditions thereby allowing for treatment based on each specific individuals needs. Through this approach one single ailment such as a headache may have many treatment approaches based on the individual and the specific type of headache which is involved. Further TCM philosophy emphasizes the fact that illness/imbalances change during their course and modifications to treatment approaches are frequently required, sometimes on a daily basis.

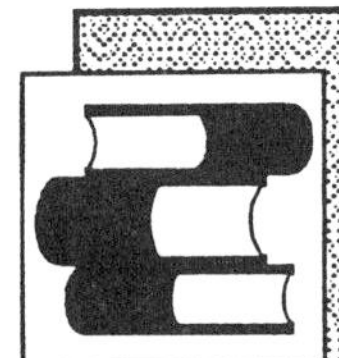

Theory
Level II, Lesson 2

Eating and drinking to cure illness and prolong life – Part 4: the apple.

Energetic Nature of Food: The apple has a sour and slightly sweet taste, is neutral in nature, and non-poisonous. The apple works through the Stomach and Spleen meridians.

Action: The action of the apple is to tonify the Heart, nourish the Lungs, dissolve phlegm, quench thirst and dissolve inflammation. The apple tonifies the whole body's Qi. (Note: To tonify means to promote the proper function of the organ meridians. Such improved function involves nourishing, supplementing, fortifying, etc.)

Indications: The apple is useful for people with a lack of Qi in their internal organs, indigestion, constipation, high blood pressure, minor diarrhea and dry throat and mouth.

Preparations

Note: continue until condition improves or as needed.

1. To treat minor diarrhea:
   - Use 10g dehydrated apple powder, mix with lukewarm water to make a thick paste; take 10g (2 to 3 tablespoons), 2 or 3 times daily (slightly Yang preparation).

2. To soften bowel movement:
   - Eat 1 or 2 apples daily on an empty Stomach (slightly Yin preparation).

3. To treat indigestion and nausea:
   - Eat 1 apple after a meal.

4. To lower high blood pressure:
   - Eat 250g apples (1 or 2 apples), 3 times a day every day.

5. To treat an infant's digestive problems:
   - Skin and thinly slice apples, cook in double boiler until soft, then mash with spoon to make applesauce. Use as food for an infant; coats intestines to slow diarrhea and indigestion caused by diarrhea. Helps to quench thirst and nourish the Spleen.

It is important to remember that the combination of foods and the manner in which they are prepared can effect their energy. For example:

Yin – –	Yin –	Neutral	Yang +	Yang + +
	Apple from refrigerator	Apple, room temperature	Apple, cooked	Apple cooked with cinnamon (Yang)
	White ginseng (Yin) congee	Plain rice congee	Red ginseng (Yang) congee	Red ginseng congee with ginger (Yang)

Related to this discussion is the fact that if you are trying to create balance using food, you can reverse the effect you are seeking by what you eat. For example if you eat Yang red ginseng congee to gather Yang and then drink Yin green leaf tea, you would most likely negate the effect you are seeking.

Method
Level II, Lesson 2

The basic fundamentals of Qigong-breath work

Exercise objective: To expand and contract the sun's energy — this expands on the exercise begun in Level II, Lesson 1. This exercise begins to teach the student how to protect themselves. This exercise is also called: "Moving the Sun Through the Day."

When is exercise performed: This exercise changes this week by adding an additional movement. The exercise learned in Lesson 1 is totally replaced by the exercise described below.

1. Hands are in the inverted triangle, it is 6am as described in Lesson 1. Inhale and move the hands upward from Dantien until thumbs reach solar plexus. As you move upward, change the time to 12 noon, a hot noon sun.

2. Exhale and expand the hands outward. As you do so picture yourself in the center of the hot noon sun. The sun is solid. As you count to 9, the layers of the sun thicken around you. During this counting, the breathing is natural. This Lesson begins to teach protection. That is by learning to surround yourself with powerful Yang energy you can "protect" yourself from outside energies which do not feel good. After counting to nine, return the hands and sun to the solar plexus position (thumbs at solar plexus, triangle pointed downward).

3. Move hands down to Dantien as the sun sets, it is 6 pm — 1/2 sun, 1/2 water. As you count to 9, mentally move from the 6pm visualization to the 6 am visualization. Hands remain in inverted triangle at Dantien.

4. Repeat exercise 9-36 times.

5. When completed begin meditation on the 6am picture of half sun, half water.
   - Note: Remember Level II, Lesson 1 is now omitted and this Lesson is practiced.

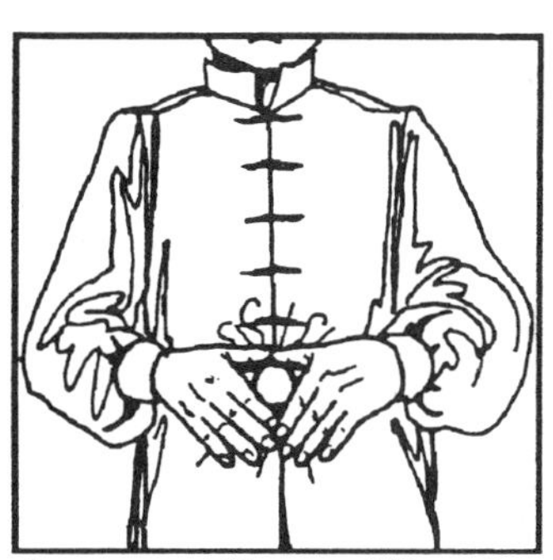
6 a.m. — 1/2 sun, 1/2 water

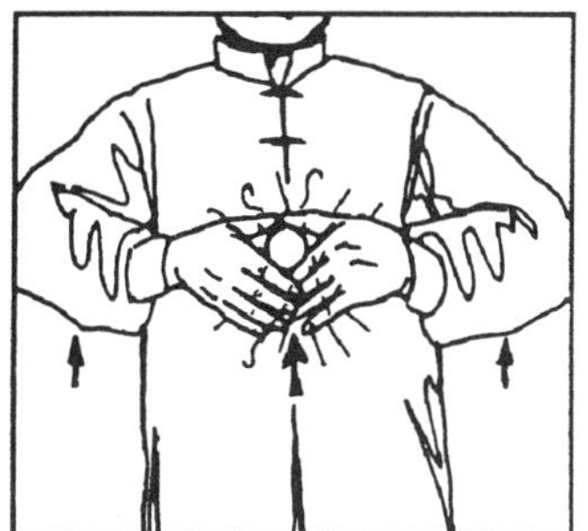
12 noon — hot noon sun

Exhale & expand the hot noon sun

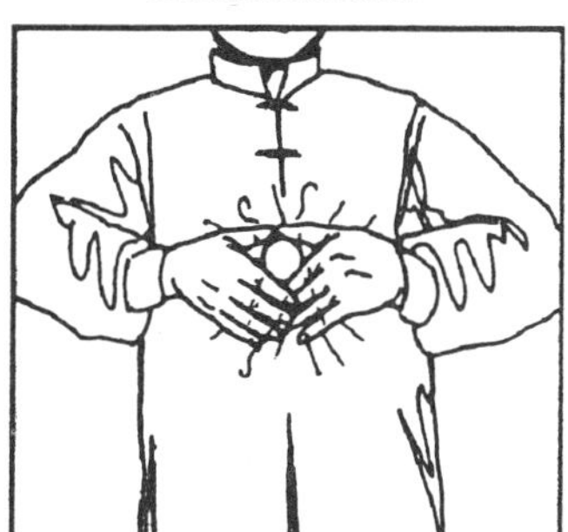
Inhale & draw the hot noon sun back to the solar plexus

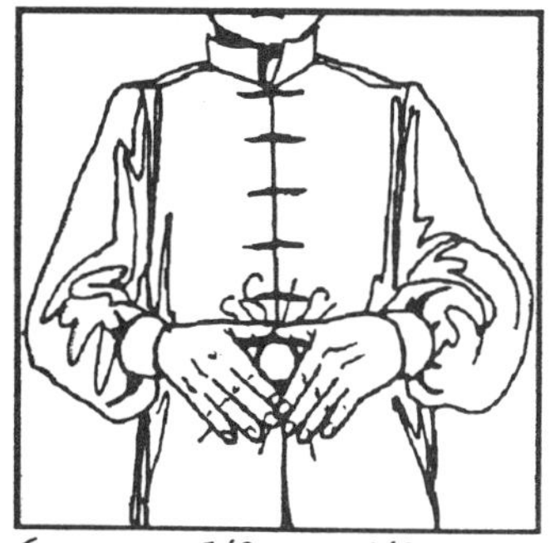
6 p.m. — 1/2 sun, 1/2 water

This Week's Sequence of Practice

1. Wash
2. Gather the Yang/Hot Noon Sun
3. Gather the Yin/Earth's Negative Waters
4. Heart and Kidney in Harmony
5. Bring Heaven, Man and Earth Together for Harmony
6. Unite the Earth and Sky in the Body
7. Bring the Morning Sun
8. Expand and Contract the Sun
9. Move the Sun Through the Day
10. Meditate
11. Quick or Full Close

Student Journal

What is well rooted cannot be disturbed.
What is well grasped cannot fall away.
— Tao Teh Ching

Extra Thoughts – movement and non-movement

Qigong is usually divided into two categories, movement (active) and non-movement (still). Reclining, sitting and standing forms of practice, where there is no visible external movement, are referred to as non-movement Qigong. Examples of *Xuan Ming Dao* Qigong Level I and II meditation, are representative of non-movement Qigong. The walking, *"five animal,"* Tai Chi Qigong and freestyle movement approaches to Qigong all belong to the category of movement Qigong. Other examples of movement Qigong include *Xuan Ming Dao* Level III through Level VII, the *"through the extremities"* methods.

The word "non-movement" is somewhat misleading. The term implies that no motion is occurring during the practice. This is however not the case. Non-movement Qigong is not completely motionless. Although there appears to be no movement from an exterior view, activity is occurring internally. For example, in standing Qigong during meditation, when looking at the person performing the meditation, they appear to be standing in the same spot without moving. But it is noted that after a period of time in the meditation, the person's body will create heat, referred to as "border heat." This heat, sometimes accompanied by sweating, is a manifestation of the organs being exercised. It is in this respect that non-movement and movement Qigong are similar. They both achieve the same goal, they serve the same purpose; that is to exercise, strengthen and tonify the internal organs, and open the channels. Both types of Qigong are necessary to provide balance in the practice.

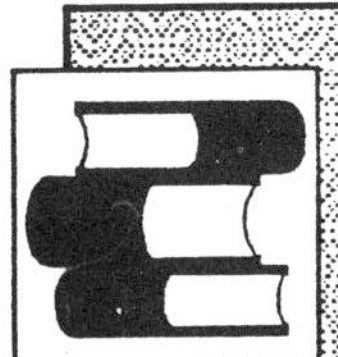

Theory
Level II, Lesson 3

Where the meaning of Qigong originated.

In ancient martial arts books the word Qigong is seldom mentioned. Qigong was not the term used, although the movements and breathing practices existed. The earliest mention of Qigong was during the Tsin dynasty (265-420 AD) by a Tao Si (teacher) named Hou Sun, who briefly mentioned the topic but did not explain it. It was not until the end of the Ching dynasty (1644-1911 AD) that a book was written with a chapter specifically devoted to Qigong. Still there was little mention of Qigong until 1934 when at a hospital in the city of Hong Chow, Dong Ho wrote three books entitled: *Chi Kung Treatments – Special Treatment for Tuberculosis.* Still, not much attention was paid to the subject.

In 1955, the Tong San Chi Kung Treatment Center was established. This hospital was built for government dignitaries and rich and famous people. But not until 1958, when the hospital's director Lo Qua Gin wrote a book called *Chi Kung Treatment – Internal Nourishing Kung,* did people begin to pay attention to the subject of Qigong. This book became one of the top sellers in China. The credit for the success of this book and the spread of the term 'Qigong' should go to the government dignitaries and the rich and famous people who received successful treatment through these methods and were cured. News of the hospital and the success of its treatments spread throughout China and the wonders of Qigong became public information. Finally in 1979, the government started to unify the practices of Qigong as practiced throughout various areas of China and a Qigong Association was formed.

Qigong has various uses including medicinal, martial arts and religious. There are three major aspects of Qigong:

- Tu Na (吐纳), breathing;
- Tao Yin (导引), energy movement, generally with physical movement;
- Meditation
  - Jo Chan (坐禅), sitting meditation; and
  - Moin San (冥想), still meditation.

Method
Level II, Lesson 3

The basic fundamentals of Qigong-breath work

Exercise objective: To tonify organs, train the energy — this expands on the exercise begun in Level II, Lesson 2

When is exercise performed: In place of Level II, Lessons 1 and 2.

1. You have just returned the morning sun to the Dantien following the expansion and contraction of the energy exercise. Pause a moment and think of the Dantien. Change the image in the Dantien of the morning sun to a picture of half sun, half water. Hands are in inverted triangle. Move hands from Dantien up the left side for the male or the right side for the female to the solar plexus, changing the time to 12 noon, and the visualization to the hot noon sun.

6 a.m. — 1/2 sun, 1/2 water

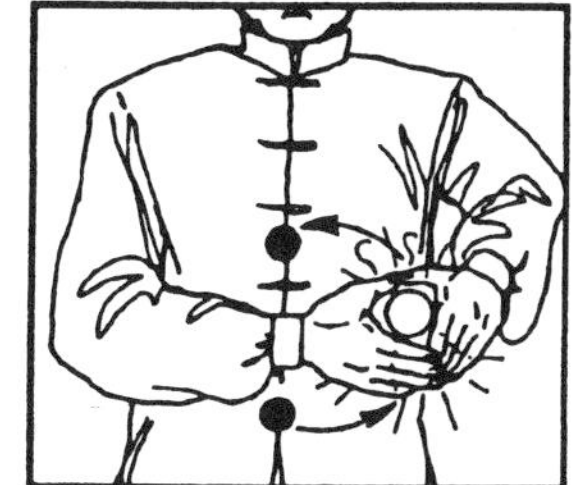

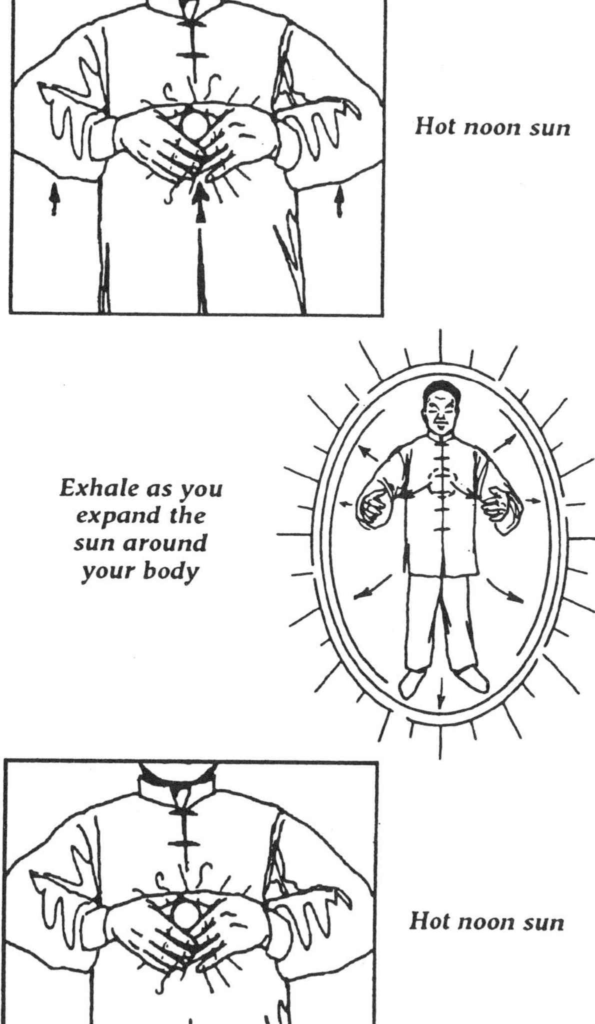

Hot noon sun

Exhale as you expand the sun around your body

Hot noon sun

2. When the thumbs are at the solar plexus, expand the hands. As this is done, think of expanding the hot noon sun. After the sun is expanded, count to nine as you increase the layers of protection of the hot noon sun around the body. As you expand you exhale. While counting to nine, breathing is natural. Remember that the sun is solid and you are in the center of the sun.

3. While inhaling contract the hands back so thumbs are again at the solar plexus.

- Note: As the hands move, the energy is moving through the center of the body, not on the surface.

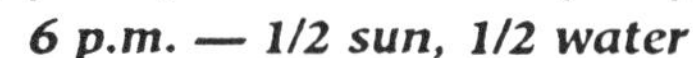

6 p.m. — 1/2 sun, 1/2 water

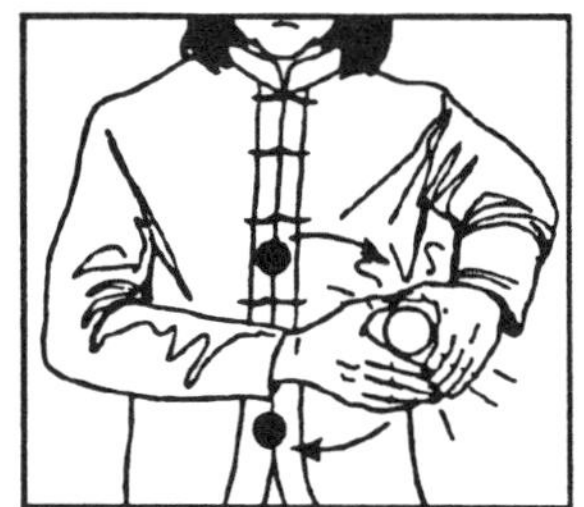

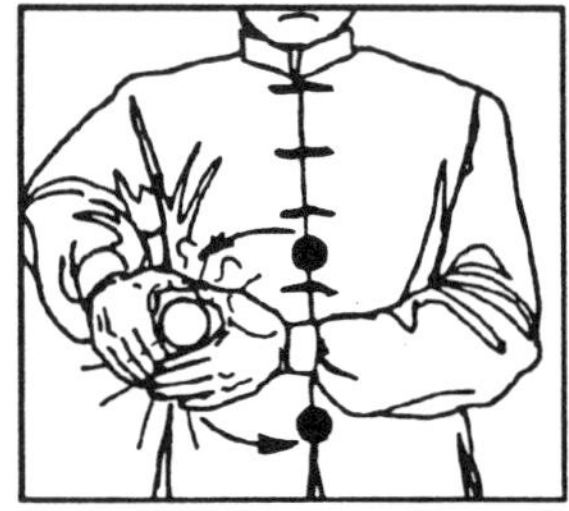

4. While exhaling move the hands down the right side for the male and the left side for the female to the Dantien. It is now 6pm and you see the half sun, half water picture in the Dantien. The characteristics of the 6pm scene are as described in the Chart in Level II, Lesson 1. Inhale as you view the 1/2 sun, 1/2 water picture. Now exhale and expand the hands outward, as you do so, expand the half sun, half water picture to circle the body. You are its center. The sun surrounds the top of your body and you are standing in the water from the naval down. Count to nine. Feel the layers of protection of the half sun, half water picture thicken.

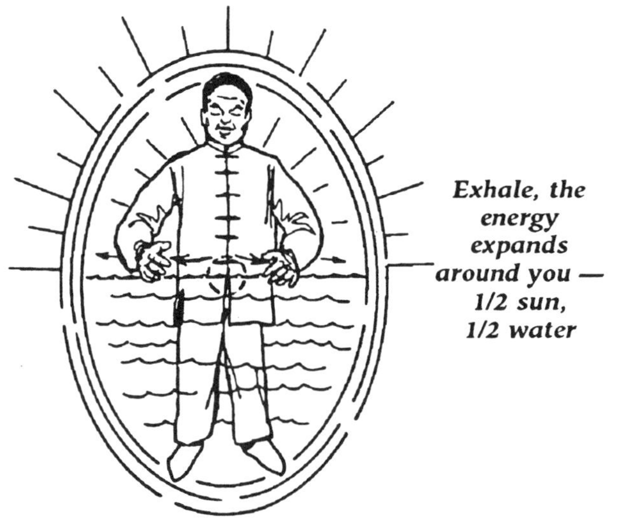

Exhale, the energy expands around you — 1/2 sun, 1/2 water

5. Inhale and draw the half sun, half water picture inward returning it to the Dantien.

6. Now count to 9 as you move from 6pm to 6am. Hands remain in inverted triangle at Dantien.

7. Repeat exercise 3 to 36 times.

8. When done begin the meditation on the visualization of the 6am half sun, half water picture.

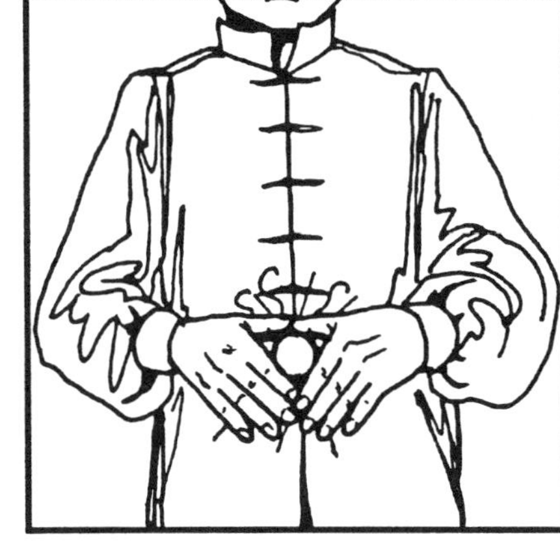

6 p.m. — 1/2 sun, 1/2 water. Now person mentally moves from 6 p.m. to 6 a.m. and begins Day 2.

Notes: (1) In doing the exercise you move up the right side (female), or left side (male) in going from the Dantien to the upper position. Move down the opposite side in returning to the Dantien. (2) Level II, Lessons 1 and 2 are now omitted and Lesson three, which combines the prior two Lessons, is only practiced. (3) Two protection mechanisms were taught. The first was the hot noon sun. This is the protection which will most often be used because of its intense Yang nature and strength. The second protection was the half sun/half-water image. This protection might be useful in an excessively Yang environment, such as a hot summer day. (4) There may be days when you will need to modify the temperature of the hot noon sun slightly in order to be comfortable.

This Week's Sequence of Practice

1. Wash
2. Gather the Yang/Hot Noon Sun
3. Gather the Yin/Earth's Negative Waters
4. Heart and Kidney in Harmony
5. Bring Heaven, Man and Earth Together for Harmony
6. Unite the Earth and Sky in the Body
7. Bring the Morning Sun
8. Expand and Contract the Sun
9. Move the Sun Through the Day
10. Meditate
11. Quick or Full Close

Student Journal

If the Tao is defined, it is not the Tao.
— Tao Teh Ching

Extra Thoughts – the components of Qigong

It can be considered that there are three parts to Qigong method study:

1. Movement:
   A. Physical Movement — The body must be kept physically active and strong. Physical movement also assists gathering energy.
   B. Energy Movement — This involves the ability to gather energy and move or "lead" the energy through the body. All of the exercises involve the use of energy or Qi in some form. One can view the self as an energy body. In Qigong one learns to feel and train their energy body. Everyone possesses energy or Qi. The level and quantity may vary, and some may have intensified their energy and ability to work with their energy through study, but everyone has the capacity to use and direct the energy in their body for specific self-health uses.
2. Meditation — Meditation is an extremely important part of the practice. It is the time when the focus is turned inward, when the energy is allowed to do its work, to tonify the body, its organs, the spirit, etc.
3. Breathing — Breathing assists all of the other aspects of the Qigong practice. It is an essential part of the practice and serves as both a support and a spur to the physical movement, leading of the energy, and meditation. Breathing naturally and in a relaxed manner helps the Qi to move freely and in an uninhibited manner.

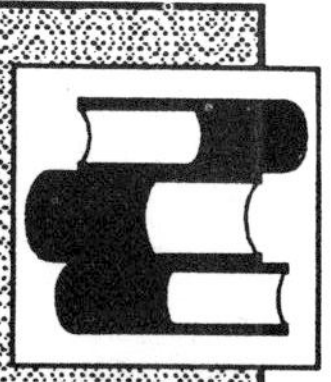

Theory
Level II, Lesson 4

Eating and drinking to cure illness and prolong life – Part 5: milk.

Energetic Nature of Food: The taste of milk is slightly sweet and it is negative, or Yin.

Meridians: Milk works through the Lung and Stomach meridians.

Explanation: Milk is a healthy drink. Its protein contains less cholesterol than meat and eggs, and it helps lower cholesterol in the body. Milk neutralizes Stomach acid, helping with bleeding ulcers and intestine. Sour milk products (such as yogurt) can control the Liver, so it does not produce cholesterol. Sour milk products also work to decrease cholesterol in the blood and clear the arteries.

Action: The action of milk is to give a weak person energy. It helps dissolve the poisons in the body and assists with bowel movements. It is good for Stomach cancer, high blood pressure and strokes.

Indications: Milk helps coat and settle the Stomach; it is good for constipation and after birth for a woman. It quenches thirst, helps bleeding Stomach and intestines, and is good for insomnia.

Preparations
Note: continue until condition improves or as needed.

✸ 1. To promote sleep:
- A cup of hot milk before going to sleep helps one sleep better and calms the nerves.

✸ 2. To treat constipation:
- Mix 250cc of milk with 100g of honey and scald. Drink warm mixture in the morning on an empty Stomach. This helps constipation and softens bowel movement.

✸ 3. To treat indigestion:
- Mix 200cc of milk, 5cc fresh ginger juice (add sugar to taste) and scald together. Drink warm to help upset Stomach, vomiting and acidic Stomach. The ginger (Yang) is added to balance the milk (Yin).

✸ 4. To protect against food poisoning:
- 500cc milk, cold — drink straight down; coats Stomach to protect from poisoning.

Method
Level II, Lesson 4

How the absorption of Qi massages the body/deep wash

Exercise objective: To cleanse the whole body. Lesson 4 is intended to cleanse the head, neck, shoulders, and arms/hands. This exercise is good for releasing/cleansing, improving the circulation, clearing the channels, and calming the self.

When is exercise performed: As part of normal Qigong practice or as needed by the individual. An example of an instance when a person might want to perform this exercise is after visiting a hospital or sick person. This exercise is normally performed at the beginning of Qigong practice to cleanse and relax the body. This exercise generally comes after the Level I washing exercise. This exercise is excellent for relaxation and a person can perform the exercise while thinking "relax" instead of, or in addition to, the water. If practiced outside of the normal full practice, this exercise should always be followed by bringing a morning sun and meditating for a short time followed by one of the closes. This is necessary since any wash is generally a form of "release," and a student should bring good, new energy in after releasing or cleansing "bad" energy.

- Note: This is a three part Lesson taught over this Lesson and the next two.

The Dazhui point is introduced in this Lesson.

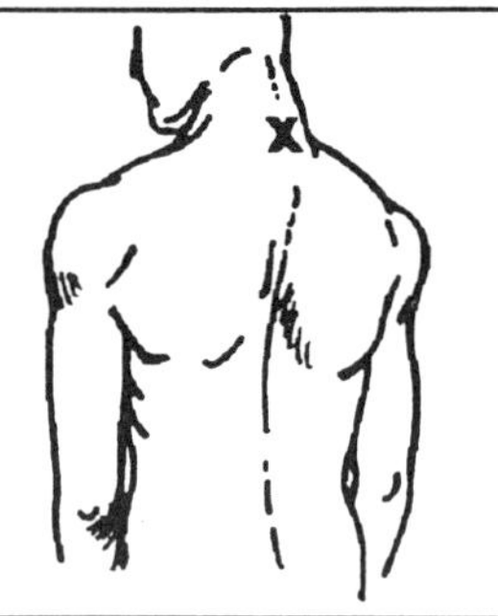	**Dazhui** 	This point is located on the back below the prominence of the 7th cervical vertebra. It is approximately at the level of the shoulders. Translated into English it means Large Vertebra. It is located on the GV or DU Channel and is Acupoint DU 14.

- A. Begin with hands at side.
- B. Visualize a mass of water coming as a shower.
- C. Inhale the water to the Baihui point. Open the Baihui point.
- D. Pour the water into the Baihui point.

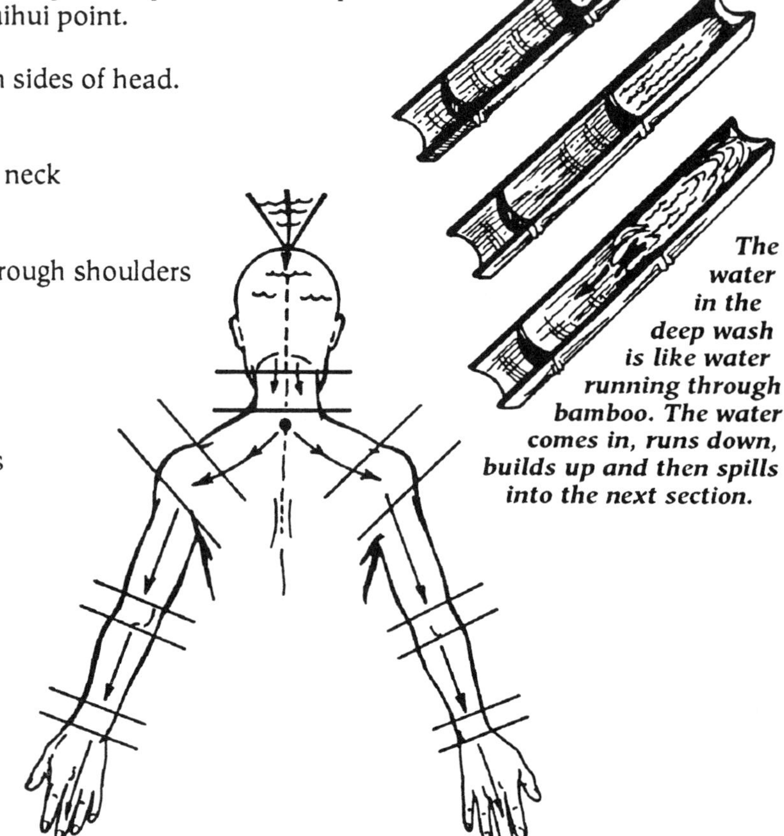

The water in the deep wash is like water running through bamboo. The water comes in, runs down, builds up and then spills into the next section.

Tip of the middle finger

1. Exhale water down inside to both sides of head.
   Inhale, hold

2. Exhale water to both sides of the neck
   Inhale, hold

3. Exhale water from Dazhui out through shoulders
   Inhale, hold

4. Exhale water to shoulder joints
   Inhale, hold

5. Exhale water through upper arms
   Inhale, hold

6. Exhale water through elbows
   Inhale, hold

7. Exhale water through lower arms
   Inhale, hold

8. Exhale water through wrists
   Inhale, hold

9. Exhale water through hands
   Inhale, hold

10. Finally concentrate all the water in the tip of the middle finger of each hand. Concentrate on visualizing the water in the tip of the middle fingers for 1 to 3 minutes. The middle finger is associated with the Pericardium, by concentrating on this point, we tonify the Pericardium and Heart.
    - Note: Exhale as the water moves down to the next body part. Inhale, hold the water. As you complete each exhale and inhale, you can also think of relaxing.

11. This exercise should be done 3 times.

12. If completing in regular practice session, begin Level I exercises.
    If completing outside practice, bring a morning sun, meditate for a short time, close.

This Week's Sequence of Practice

1. Wash
2. Deep Wash, Head, Shoulders, Arms, Hands
3. Gather the Yang/Hot Noon Sun
4. Gather the Yin/Earth's Negative Waters
5. Heart and Kidney in Harmony
6. Bring Heaven, Man and Earth Together for Harmony
7. Unite the Earth and Sky in the Body
8. Bring the Morning Sun
9. Expand and Contract the Sun
10. Move the Sun Through the Day
11. Meditate
12. Quick or Full Close

Student Journal

How do I know the world?
By knowing myself.
— Tao Teh Ching

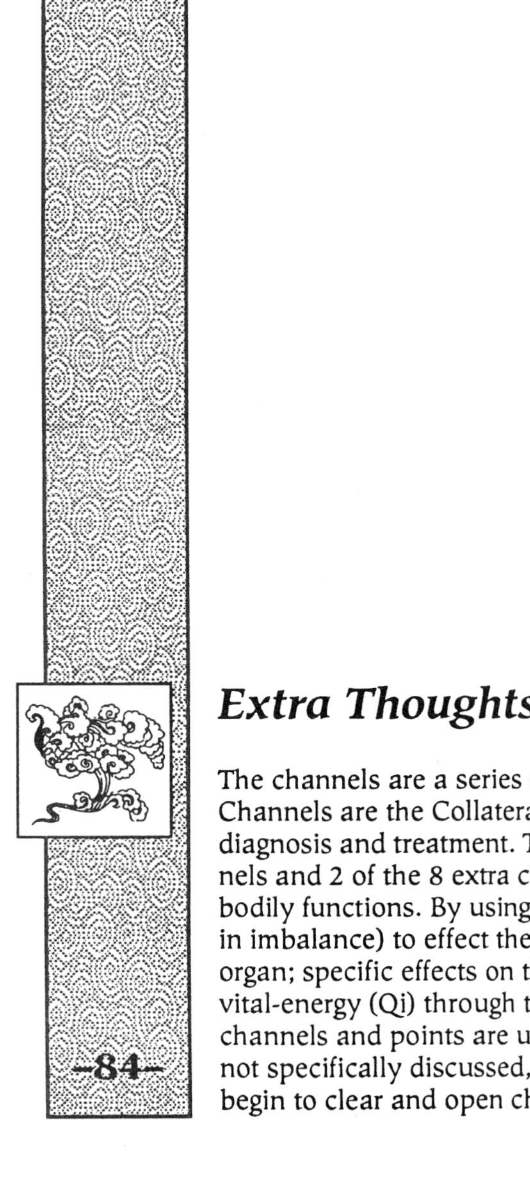

Extra Thoughts – meridian/channel theory

The channels are a series of networks or pathways running throughout the body. Stemming from the Channels are the Collaterals. The Channels and Collaterals within the body form another basis for diagnosis and treatment. There are 12 regular channels and 8 extra channels. The 12 regular channels and 2 of the 8 extra channels contain specific points which are directly related to organs and bodily functions. By using these points an impact can be made upon the necessary areas (i.e. areas in imbalance) to effect the desired result. Every point has specific therapeutic effects on the related organ; specific effects on the body areas covered by the channel; and a general effect on the body's vital-energy (Qi) through the channel complex. As skill and knowledge advance in Qigong, the channels and points are used to treat specific imbalance situations. In Level I and II, channels are not specifically discussed, however, many of the exercises are designed to automatically work to begin to clear and open channels.

Theory
Level II, Lesson 5

How Qigong was originally introduced.

Qigong was introduced to the people through four different philosophies: the way of the Tao; Confucianism; Taoism (religious); and Buddhism. The first two, the philosophy of the Tao and Confucianism, are concerned with nature and philosophical thought, and are not to be confused with the latter two, which are primarily religious in nature. In each case, the practices were handed down to the people to help make the body strong and healthy and to help satisfy a self-need (i.e., I do this because it is good).

Over time people gathered information from their Qigong experiences. These experiences came from different styles and systems, and were developed for different body types. The result was over 1,000 different ways to practice Qigong. Its applications are analogous to those of medicine, i.e., different cures for different problems. Modern Qigong is rich in experience, there is more than enough to learn and practice. All of this can be credited to the ancient peoples' efforts; their experimentation, refinement and definition of Qigong.

Lao Tzu, author of the Tao Teh Ching

Method
Level II, Lesson 5

How the absorption of Qi massages the body/deep wash

Exercise objective: To cleanse the whole body. This Lesson is intended to cleanse the back of the body.

When is exercise performed: As part of normal Qigong practice, after Level II, Lesson 4 or as needed by individual.

The Huiyin point is introduced in this exercise.

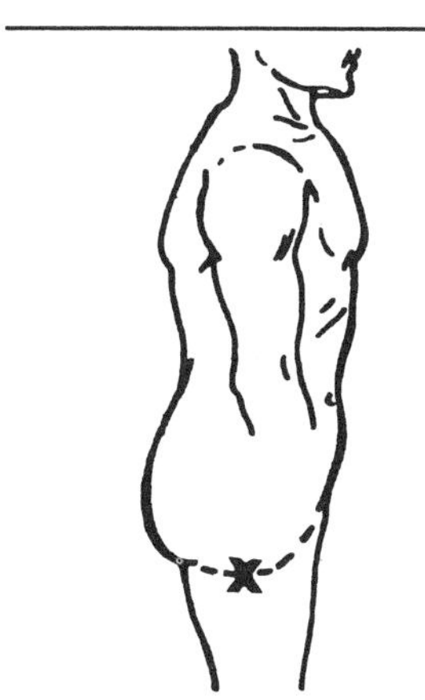	**Huiyin**  	Found on the perineum, at the midpoint between the posterior border of scrotum and anus in males, and between the posterior commissure of large labia and anus in females. Translated into English it means Crossing Genitalia. It is located on the CV or Ren Channel and is Acupoint CV 1.

- A. Begin with hands at side.
- B. Visualize a mass of water showering down.
- C. Inhale the water to the Baihui point. Open the Baihui point.
- D. Pour the water into the Baihui point.

1. Exhale water down the back of the head.
   Inhale, hold
2. Exhale water to the back of the neck
   Inhale, hold
3. Exhale water from the back of the neck to the Mingmen (i.e. upper back)
   Inhale, hold
4. Exhale water from Mingmen to Huiyin (i.e. lower back)
   Inhale, hold
5. Exhale water through back of upper legs
   Inhale, hold
6. Exhale water through whole knees
   Inhale, hold
7. Exhale water through back of lower legs
   Inhale, hold
8. Exhale water through whole ankles
   Inhale, hold
9. Exhale water through bottom of feet to toes
   Inhale, hold
10. Concentrate the water in Yongquan for 1 to 3 minutes. The Yongquan is associated with the Kidney channel. By concentrating on this point we are tonifying the Kidney.
11. This exercise should be done 3 times. Remember first you do Head and Shoulders (per Lesson 4), then you do the back. That is one set. Do 3 sets.
12. If completing in regular practice session, begin Level I exercises.
    If completing outside practice, bring a morning sun, meditate for a short time, close.

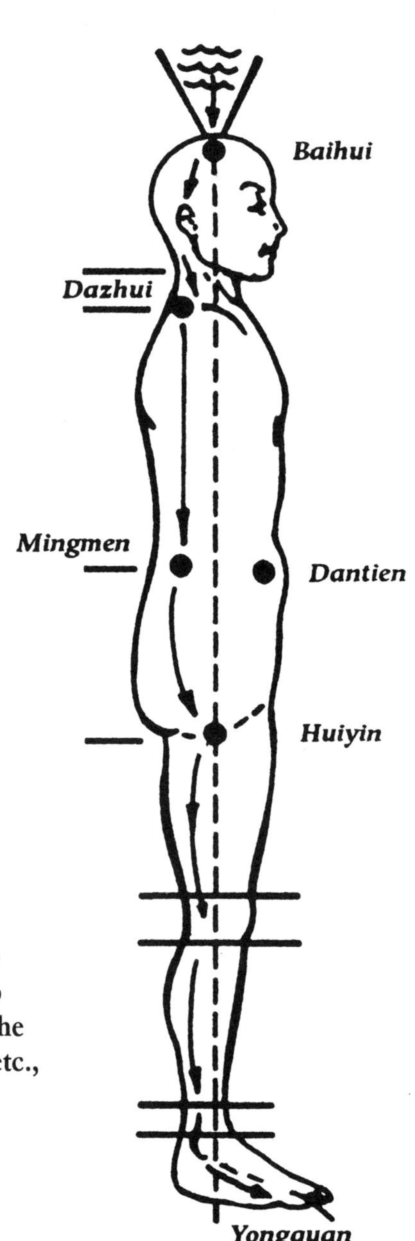

- Notes: (1) The Dazhui is the Acupoint that separates the bottom of the neck from the top of the back in the Deep Wash. (2) When water is moved to Mingmen, it means the water should be moved to Mingmen *level*, Huiyin *level*, etc., not to the specific Acupoint.

This Week's Sequence of Practice

1. Wash
2. Deep Wash, Head, Shoulders, Arms, Hands
   Deep Wash, Back of Body
3. Gather the Yang/Hot Noon Sun
4. Gather the Yin/Earth's Negative Waters
5. Heart and Kidney in Harmony
6. Bring Heaven, Man and Earth Together for Harmony
7. Unite the Earth and Sky in the Body
8. Bring the Morning Sun
9. Expand and Contract the Sun
10. Move the Sun Through the Day
11. Meditate
12. Quick or Full Close

Student Journal

If you know how to live in the flow of the way (Tao),
You will meet no obstacles on the road which cannot be overcome.
For in you the world will find no space to attack.
— Tao Teh Ching

Extra Thoughts – use reason in Qigong practice

It must be recognized that Qigong study requires a balance of active practice and reasonable rest. Qigong can be compared to cooking rice; first you boil the rice and then you allow it to simmer. Qigong can also be viewed as Yang as the practice and Yin as the nourishing; and/or the active methods of Qigong as the movement phase of Qigong and meditation as the non-movement phase.

This concept is important for all, but particularly for the person who has a chronic sickness. When a person first practices Qigong, they may think that Qigong is a quick method to eliminate their sickness completely. They therefore practice day and night, for long periods of time, thinking that they will strengthen their Qi through this approach. However, this approach will not lead to good results and sometimes this method may actually result in a worsening of the illness. From the start of Qigong study, that is Level I, the student is advised that they must practice according to their own body condition and Qigong knowledge and training. Usually a person should practice until they feel "good." Practice should never continue to the point of exhaustion or even to the point where the person begins to feel fatigued. If the student feels tired or the spirit starts to "drop," practice should be discontinued (that is proceed in the correct order to the close). If the practice is not stopped, backfires may occur.

Another example is that when you practice Qigong it is like eating rice. Normally a person might eat two bowls of rice at a time, three times a day. With this quantity their body feels comfortable and nourished. But if they think they must eat more to fight off an illness, and they eat four bowls of rice at a time, six times a day, they will not only feel tired from overeating because they have doubled the amount their body needs, but they will also effect their internal system. The digestive system will have to work harder to process and absorb the food, and the body may reject through the excretory system what it is supposed to absorb as a source of energy. The "extra" rice has therefore been of no use and in fact has caused extra work and stress for the body. Qigong teaches the student to develop sensitivity to their energy and their body. In practice, as in all things, that sensitivity should direct the student.

Theory
Level II, Lesson 6

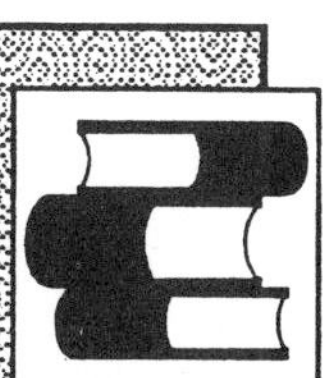

Eating and drinking to cure illness and prolong life – Part 6: beef.

Energetic Nature of Food: The topic of this Lesson is beef. The taste of beef is slightly sweet, the action is warm, and slightly positive or Yang in nature. Beef is slightly toxic, with certain side effects.

Meridians: Beef works through the Stomach and Spleen meridians, nourishing the Qi of these organs.

Explanation: Beef is enjoyed for its delicious taste. It is a rich source of protein, containing twice as much by weight as pork. It is rich in vitamins and low in fat, and cholesterol. It contains the 12 essential amino acids needed for protein production in the body. It is suitable as a food for obese people, people with high blood pressure, Heart problems, and diabetes. Beef gives energy and builds body tissue.

Action: Beef strengthens bones and ligaments, and generally nourishes internal organs and systems. It reduces internal dampness, eliminating excess fluid like water on the knee or swollen feet. Beef also strengthens the waist and knees.

Indications: Beef is especially suitable for weaker people, warming the Stomach and strengthening the Spleen. However, for those with skin problems, beef will exacerbate eruptions. Beef may also aggravate Liver problems (e.g., hepatitis) and Kidney infections or cause them to re-occur.

Contra-indications: Beef should be avoided by people with skin problems; such as boils, acne, and pimples.

Preparations
Note: continue until condition improves or as needed.

1. To strengthen the body during sickness:
   - Cook 60g of very lean ground beef in 1 cup hot water (not boiling, 60-70° C) for 10 minutes, remove the beef, and boil the remaining liquid into a broth. Drink to strengthen the blood and Stomach. Good for recuperation, Stomach, and Spleen. Discard beef, drink broth.

2. To treat hemorrhoids or swelling of feet or face (edema):
   - Place 100g beef in 2 bowls water. Bring to a boil and boil for 5 minutes. Then reduce heat and simmer to reduce liquid to one bowl, and make a strong broth. Drink to treat swollen conditions. This preparation is also good for the Spleen. Beef can be eaten or discarded.

3. To treat day sweats, Qi deficiency:
   - 250g of beef, 30g Huang Qi (黄芪), 30g Dang Shen(党参), 30g Wei Shan Yao (淮山药), 30g Fu Xiao Mai (浮小麦), 15g Bai Zhu (白术), 10g fresh ginger, 10 pieces Da Zao(大枣). Cook together as soup, salt to taste, eat beef and drink liquid. Discard herbs.

4. To treat Lung deficiencies:
   - Simmer 250g sliced beef with 25g fresh ginger in 2-3 bowls water until 80% done, then add 500g pumpkin squash with skin; cook until squash is soft, add salt to taste. Strengthens and lowers inflammation in Lungs, relieves aches, helps expel fluid from the Lungs.

Method
Level II, Lesson 6

How the absorption of Qi massages the body/deep wash

Exercise objective: To cleanse the whole body. This Lesson is intended to cleanse the front of the body.

When is exercise performed: As part of normal Qigong practice. As needed by individual.

- A. Begin with hands at side
- B. Visualize a mass of water showering down
- C. Inhale water to Baihui point, open the Baihui point
- D. Pour the water into the Baihui point

1. Exhale water down the front of the head and face.
   Inhale, hold

2. Exhale water to the front of the neck
   Inhale, hold

3. Exhale water from the neck to the Dantien (i.e. front of upper body)
   Inhale, hold

4. Exhale water from Dantien to Huiyin (i.e. front of lower body)
   Inhale, hold

5. Exhale water through front of upper legs
   Inhale, hold

6. Exhale water through whole knees
   Inhale, hold

7. Exhale water through front of lower legs
   Inhale, hold

8. Exhale water through whole ankles
   Inhale, hold

9. Exhale water through top of feet to toes
   Inhale, hold

10. Finally move the water to the tip and end of big toes, concentrate water in the big toe nail areas for 1 to 3 minutes. Acupoints (associated with the Spleen and Liver) are located on each side of the toe nail. By concentrating on these points we tonify the Spleen and Liver.

11. If completing in regular practice session, begin Level I exercises.
    If completing outside practice, bring a morning sun, meditate for a short time, close.
    - Note: remember, exercise is performed in sequence. That is, do head and shoulders, etc., then back, then front. This is one set. Do 1-3 sets as part of your regular practice.

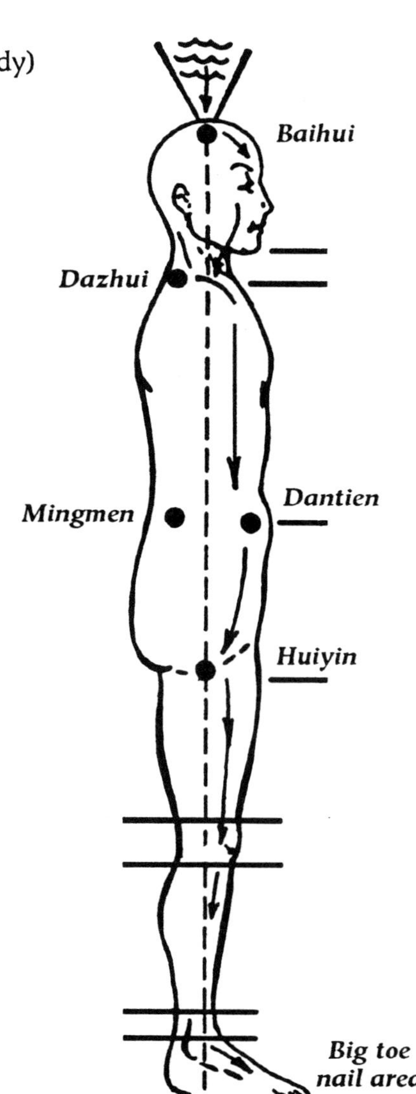

This Week's Sequence of Practice

1. Wash

2. Deep Wash, Head, Shoulders, Arms, Hands
   Deep Wash, Back of Body
   Deep Wash, Front of Body

3. Gather the Yang/Hot Noon Sun

4. Gather the Yin/Earth's Negative Waters

5. Heart and Kidney in Harmony

6. Bring Heaven, Man and Earth Together for Harmony

7. Unite the Earth and Sky in the Body

8. Bring the Morning Sun

9. Expand and Contract the Sun

10. Move the Sun Through the Day

11. Meditate

12. Quick or Full Close

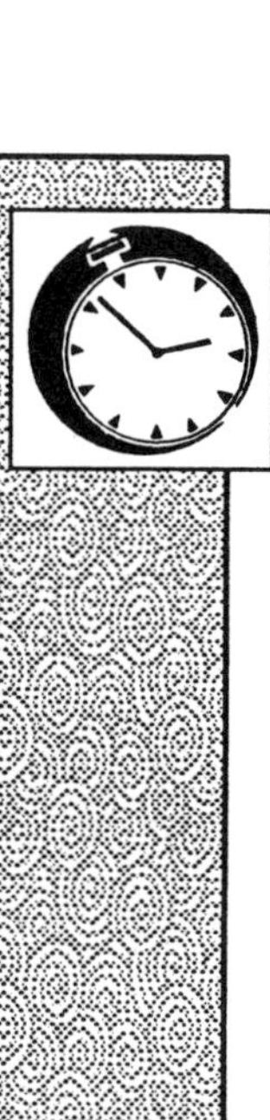

Student Journal

Learning consists in daily acquisition of information;
The practice of Tao consists in daily reduction of information.
— Tao Teh Ching

Extra Thoughts – Qi and the mind

In the practice of Qigong, Qi and the mind (thought) must be closely linked. Qi and the mind both rely on each other and work together to produce positive results. As a primary force within the body, Qi plays a critical role in the functionality of the body. Qi is not used solely to exercise the major organs, Qi also effects the channels, the blood flow, and other bodily functions. Therefore in the practice of Qigong the primary focus must be on the cultivation of Qi.

However the cultivation of Qi is not the only consideration, if a person cannot control the internal Qi, that is learn to generate, store, and maneuver the Qi throughout the entire body, it means that the mind (thought) and Qi are not in harmony. That is why in *Xuan Ming Dao* Qigong, Level I and Level II must be practiced both prior to, and in order to reach Level III, as well as other more advanced Levels. This requirement stems from the fact that Level I and II form the foundation for the entire study of Qigong. These levels have as their core principles:

1. the balancing of the body's internal Qi,
2. methods to assist the absorption of external natural Qi,
3. learning to use the mind (as the parent), to control the Qi (as the child), to benefit the whole body.

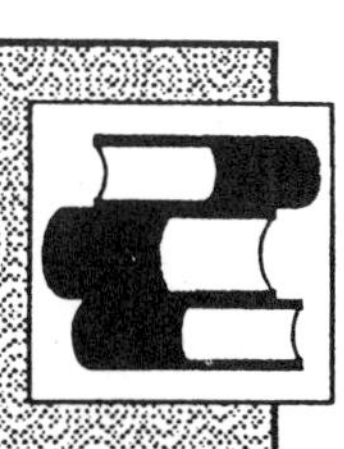

Theory
Level II, Lesson 7

Defining the Qigong doctor and Chinese medical theory.

In Chinese medical uses of Qigong, the purpose is to analyze and explore the human body, and to study its sicknesses and their prevention in a scientific way. The unique theory of Qigong healing, which was not copied from any other system, was gathered through generations of practice and study to become a rich storehouse of knowledge and information which can be used for health and longevity. The purpose of Qigong self-treatment is to manipulate the Qi in different ways to cure sickness and strengthen the body.

Qigong forms a large part of the theoretical and experiential research base which supports Chinese medical theory. The use of Qigong to cure sickness is a precious Chinese tradition, closely related to Chinese medical theory. Although Chinese medical theory uses Qigong to explain the self-healing of illness, people often forget that Qigong predated the formalization of Chinese medical theory and therefore formed the practical basis of the Chinese medical model. Recently, Chinese medicine has begun to apply the principles of modern medical theory as a research basis for the investigation and explanation of Qigong, thus using the child (Chinese Medicine) to understand the parent (Qigong).

Throughout this Workbook we have discussed Traditional Chinese Medicine (TCM) theories and principles side by side with Qigong. Varied opinions exist on their relationship. Qigong today is most often considered as a sub-set and treatment modality of TCM. However, it is important to remember that Qigong and its development predated formalized TCM and that the two systems developed differentially. Today the two are considered as closely related partially because they share many common underlaying theoretical bases (Qi, Channels, Five Element theory, etc.). However it is important to also appreciate the differences between the two practices. Qigong's focus is on energy used as a pure force for healing and wellness. TCM, on the other hand, uses acupuncture, acupressure, massage and herbs as primary treatment methods. The differences in the two studies will emerge and be explored in more depth in higher levels.

Method
Level II, Lesson 7

How Qigong strengthens the Kidneys — Kidney back massage

Exercise Objective: To strengthen and nourish the Kidney's Yang energy. This exercise is a good energy booster when tired.

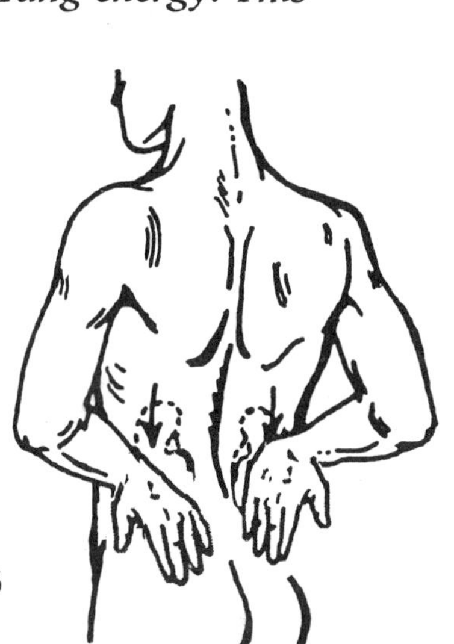

1. Think of opening the Laogong points.
2. Think of bringing energy to the Laogong points.
3. Place Laogong points (palms of hand) over Kidneys.
4. Think of inhaling energy to Laogong, exhale and think of moving the energy into the Kidneys (exhale into Kidneys, inhale new energy to Laogong) — repeat 9 to 36 times.
5. Use the hands to massage up and down. Inhale up and exhale down. The hands are moving up and down from approximately the Kidney area at the top, to the coccyx at the bottom — repeat 9 to 36 times. Think your hand inside your body while doing this exercise.
6. When massage is completed, hands stop over Kidneys, think of sealing or leaving the energy in the Kidneys while counting to 9.
   - Note: The three Kidney exercises, this one and the ones taught over the next two Lessons can be performed outside of the regular practice sessions. They are designed for use when the student feels a need to bolster their Yin and/or Yang Kidney energy.

This Week's Sequence of Practice

1. Wash
2. Deep Wash, Head, Shoulders, Hands
   Deep Wash, Back of Body
   Deep Wash, Front of Body
3. Gather the Yang/Hot Noon Sun
4. Gather the Yin/Earth's Negative Waters
5. Heart and Kidney in Harmony
6. Bring Heaven, Man and Earth Together for Harmony
7. Unite the Earth and Sky in the Body
8. Bring the Morning Sun
9. Expand and Contract the Sun
10. Move the Sun Through the Day
11. Meditate
12. Quick or Full Close
13. Kidney Back Massage

Student Journal

Keep on reducing until you reach the state of non-action.
In the state of non-action, nothing is left undone.
— Tao Teh Ching

Extra Thoughts – emptying the mind

To comprehend that our feeling that we have knowledge is ignorance. This is an important understanding. The wise man learns that he must forget his learning.

This statement is from the *Tao Teh Ching.* It would seem odd to most people since a high value is properly placed on knowledge and learning. However this statement reminds us of our need to "let go," relax, become natural — move toward and achieve harmony with the *flow of the way (the Tao).* These principles apply directly to our Qigong practice. Only through releasing ourselves and freeing the mind, body and spirit can we progress in Qigong. Seeking naturalness, quiet and relaxation, we allow the body and its energy to do the work which is required to achieve and maintain balance and harmony within ourselves and with the environment around us. Further, excessive thinking and over-analyzing your practice can be detrimental. Accepting that what is occurring in the practice (provided it is comfortable and feels right) is what should be occurring, is necessary. Sometimes thought can interfere with perception. If we fill our minds to overflowing, nothing else can get in. Insights and perception must be given "room" to occur. Emptying the mind allows this.

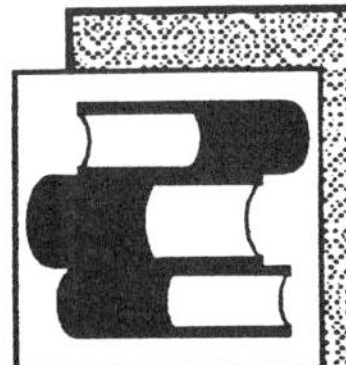

Theory
Level II, Lesson 8

Eating and drinking to cure illness and prolong life – Part 7: eggs.

Energetic Nature of Food: The topic of this Lesson is eggs. The taste of eggs is slightly sweet, and they are neutral and non-toxic.

Meridians: The egg works through the Heart, Lung, Spleen, Stomach, and Kidney meridians.

Action: The action of eggs helps insomnia, nervousness, dry cough, loss of voice, dizziness, thirst, night blindness, persistent cough, and stimulates milk production in nursing women. Eggs are also good for not enough Yin and/or a Yin deficiency resulting in sweating of the two hands or palms, bottom of the two feet, and chest (the five sweats).

Indications: Eggs help nourish the Heart, calm the nerves, strengthen the blood, tonify the Yin, neutralize a hot system, and remove toxins from the system.

Preparations
Note: continue until condition improves or as needed.

1. To rebalance women after menstrual period:
   - Boil 10g Dang Gui (当归)[angelica root] in water; add two whole eggs (in the shell), and 30g brown sugar. Cook until eggs are hard-boiled; then peel eggs and add to same water originally used to make soup. Drink to restore regularity of period and to restore blood to a healthy condition. Discard herbs.

2. To treat persistent bronchitis:
   - Scramble two eggs (do not cook), add 30g white sugar, mix with 1/2 cup hot water, drink.

3. To treat a Yin Stomach:
   - Scramble 1 egg and seven crushed peppercorns, cook and eat to treat a cold (Yin) Stomach or Stomach ulcers.

4. To treat a Yin Stomach:
   A) Hard boil egg in shell with 1/2 cup vinegar, peel and eat.
   B) Scramble and stir fry one egg with white vinegar, eat.
   C) Break egg into wine, stir and drink (do not cook).
   - Note: These preparations also help to control diarrhea.

5. To strengthen Liver and Kidneys:
   - Add 60 to 100g He Shou Wu (何首乌), to boiling water, cook about 30 minutes, cool to room temperature, add 2 or 3 whole eggs, hard boil them in the water, then peel and cook again in the same water for 30 minutes, and eat eggs and drink broth. Good for Liver and Kidneys, strengthens blood and general vitality, helps prevent dizziness, constipation, graying hair and hair loss. Also prevents wet dreams and premature ejaculation in the male, and treats vaginal yeast infections in the female. A general tonifier. Discard herbs.

6. To treat Liver deficiencies:
   - Add 15 to 30g Gou Qi Zi (枸杞子) [tiny red berries/wolf berries] (or use 100-200g fresh leaves from same plant) and 5-10 pieces Hong Zao (红枣), [a larger berry] to hot water (2-1/2 cups water to 1 egg), add 2 to 3 whole eggs and cook until hard; peel shells, return eggs to water, and simmer again for 1/2 to 1 hour. Then eat eggs and drink broth. Strengthens Liver, Kidneys, and Spleen; prevents dizziness, nervousness, insomnia, and vision problems. Herbs can be eaten.

Method
Level II, Lesson 8

How Qigong strengthens the Kidneys — Kidney teeth exercise

Exercise Objective: To strengthen the teeth, roots, and gums. To nourish the Kidney's Yin.

1. Think of bringing energy to the teeth before starting exercise.
2. Click teeth gently together in each position 36 to 100 times.
   - A. Click back teeth
   - B. Click front teeth
   - C. Click all teeth
3. Move tongue in circular motion over outside top of teeth and gums (upper and lower), move counterclockwise and then clockwise, do 18-36 times in each direction.
4. By this point in the exercise, saliva will have gathered in the mouth, push saliva back and forth through teeth 36 times.
5. Swallow saliva in three parts to Dantien
   - Note: During the practice, the saliva in the mouth will increase. This is a sign. Saliva in Chinese represents tongue and water. If the mouth has water then it is alive, if the tongue has no water then it cannot live. The tongue and water are considered a main stream of life and critical to existence. The ancient Chinese say when a person practices Qigong, saliva is produced. Saliva is referred to by several names:

     • Yu Chuan — the jade spring,
     • Gum gen — gold liquid,
     • Yu Yec — jade liquid,

     A well known Chinese author, wrote books on how to swallow the saliva so that it travels all the way down to the Dantien. The belief was that this approach could rid the five organs of backfires, that it could prolong life, cure illness, and tonify Yin. In addition, it is believed that saliva can cut down fire, assist digestion, etc. Qigong practice therefore should increase the amount of saliva, this in turn results in the positive benefits noted above. The saliva should be swallowed. As this is done visualize the saliva going all the way down to the Dantien. If there is phlegm it should be expectorated (i.e. spit it out).

This Week's Sequence of Practice

1. Kidney Teeth Exercise
2. Wash
3. Deep Wash, Head, Shoulders, Hands
   Deep Wash, Back of Body
   Deep Wash, Front of Body
4. Gather the Yang/Hot Noon Sun
5. Gather the Yin/Earth's Negative Waters
6. Heart and Kidney in Harmony
7. Bring Heaven, Man and Earth Together for Harmony
8. Unite the Earth and Sky in the Body
9. Bring the Morning Sun
10. Expand and Contract the Sun
11. Move the Sun Through the Day
12. Meditate
13. Quick or Full Close
14. Kidney Back Massage

Student Journal

To win the world,
one must lose the world.
— Tao Teh Ching

Extra Thoughts – Qigong practice and sleep

If during the practice a person falls asleep they do not need to do the close before going to sleep. During practice it is normal to fall asleep since the practice itself assists relaxation and enhances the ability to fall asleep. Practicing Qigong lying down is particularly good for those with insomnia. However, when the practitioner awakens, they must do the complete close. The 36 rotations should be completed and the hand energy rub done, prior to rising. Then the remainder of the complete close is done while sitting or standing. This approach is safest and ensures that all of the energy is returned to, and stored, in the Dantien. If it is impossible to do the complete close, the quick close can be done.

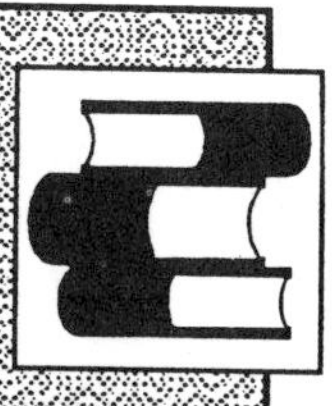

Theory
Level II, Lesson 9

The formation of Chinese medical theory.

Chinese medical theory, first formalized by the Yellow Emperor in ancient times, was developed through the interplay of intuitive conceptual thought and realistic observation. That is, practitioners over time through experimentation, and evaluation of the results of that experimentation, developed a unified approach for the utilization of the various aspects of Qigong theory and treatment. Based on the information gained, a specific body of knowledge and series of techniques which could be successfully applied to cure illness and promote longevity were developed.

According to Qigong and Chinese medical theory, a problem is diagnosed by identifying the imbalance of Yin and Yang and the inter-relationships of the five elements (wood, fire, earth, metal, and water, linked to the five principle organs; Liver, Heart, Spleen, Lung, Kidney) in the body, considered as a whole unit or system. Observing (sensing, perceiving) one's internal organs, their linkage within the energy meridians (reflected in the vascular and nervous systems), and the nature of the illness, are the starting points for determining the balance or imbalance of Yin/Yang. By knowing the theory we can monitor and adjust our practice of Qigong to balance the body's energies and eliminate our illnesses.

Method
Level II, Lesson 9

How Qigong strengths the Kidneys — Kidney foot/hand massage

Exercise Objective: To bring Yin energy to the Kidney by working with the Yongquan (K1) point.

1. Inhale energy to Laogong.

2. Place one hand on the bottom of the foot with the Laogong point over the Yongquan point. Inhale new energy to Laogong, exhale the energy into Yongquan. Repeat 9 to 36 times. This can be done on one foot or both. Do one foot at a time. The "other" hand can be placed in a comfortable position on the foot to help hold the foot.

3. Now massage the foot (think your hand inside the foot).

   A. Inhale as hand moves upward to heel.

   B. Exhale as hand moves downward to toes. Repeat 9 to 36 times.

4. Reposition the hand so the Laogong is over the Yongquan. Think of sealing/leaving the energy in Yongquan while counting to 9.

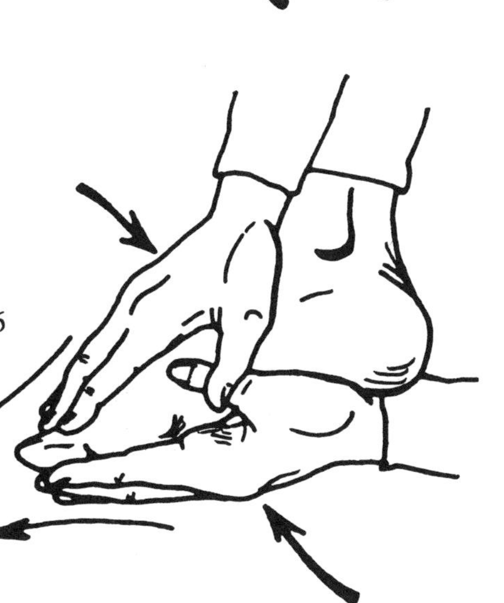

This Week's Sequence of Practice

1. Kidney Teeth Exercise
2. Wash
3. Deep Wash, Head, Shoulders, Hands
   Deep Wash, Back of Body
   Deep Wash, Front of Body
4. Gather the Yang/Hot Noon Sun
5. Gather the Yin/Earth's Negative Waters
6. Heart and Kidney in Harmony
7. Bring Heaven, Man and Earth Together for Harmony
8. Unite the Earth and Sky in the Body
9. Bring the Morning Sun
10. Expand and Contract the Sun
11. Move the Sun Through the Day
12. Meditate
13. Quick or Full Close
14. Kidney Back Massage
15. Kidney Foot Massage

Student Journal

A person must learn when enough is enough.
Such a person will always have enough.
— Tao Teh Ching

Extra Thoughts – Five Element theory

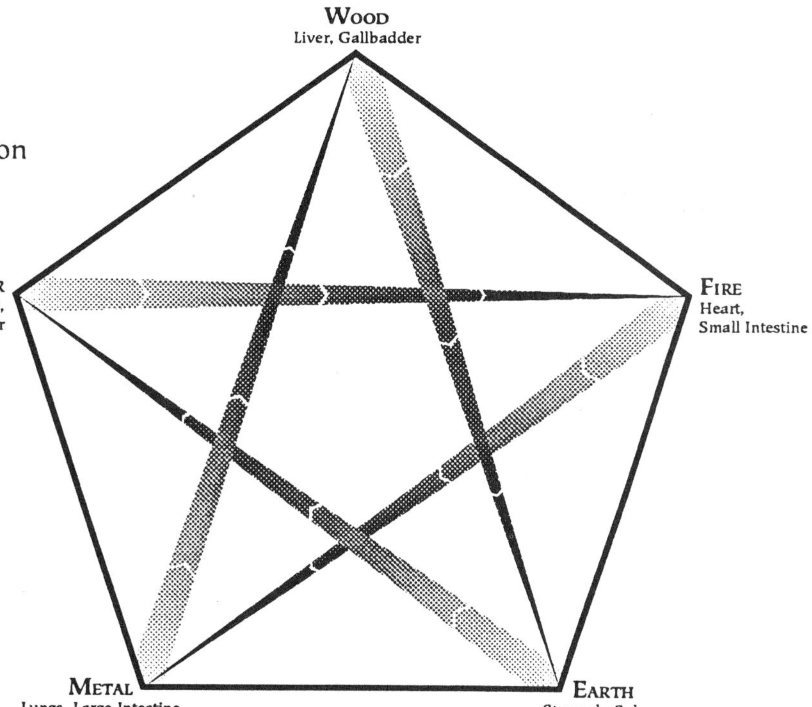

The Five Element theory is based on the five basic elements in nature as described in Chinese philosophy. The five elements are; wood (Liver/ Gall Bladder), fire (Heart/ Small Intestine), earth (Spleen/Stomach), metal (Lung/Large Intestine), and water (Kidney/Bladder). Each of these elements relates to one other element to either generate or to subjugate it. Wood generates fire; fire is subjugated by water; water generates wood; wood subjugates earth; earth generates metal; and so on. The vital human organs are seen in similar cycles, as generating and subjugating other organs. Each organ is assigned one of the five elements to describe their relationships with other organs and to assist the practitioner of Traditional Chinese Medicine in diagnosis. Over centuries of observation and speculation, the complex relationships between the organs and the internal and external forces acting upon them have resulted in a systematic method of diagnosis and treatment with ample room for the analytical ability, and the trials and errors of the individual practitioner. Chinese medicine is the product of centuries of searching for answers to human health in holistic terms. As you advance in Qigong study, Five Element theory becomes very important to both the analysis of the balance state of the body and to the development of treatment approaches. Five Element theory is therefore discussed in detail in later Levels of study.

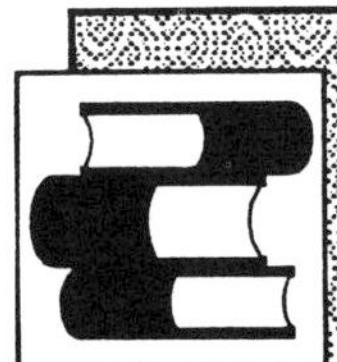

Theory
Level II, Lesson 10

Eating and drinking to cure illness and prolong life – Part 8: the potato.

Energetic Nature of Food: The taste of the potato is slightly sweet and it is neutral.

Meridians: Potatoes work through the Stomach and Large Intestine meridians.

Action: The action of the potato is to nourish the Spleen and Stomach. Potatoes also tonify the Qi.

Indications: Potatoes work internally to heal ulcers and eliminate constipation. They work externally to heal skin eruptions.

Explanation: Potatoes contain starch, protein and vitamins B and C. They also contain a small amount of solanine, a bitter poisonous crystalline alkaloid which helps eliminate cramps and reduce Stomach acid. However, too much of this chemical is toxic, causing nausea, vomiting, diarrhea and dizziness. In extreme cases it can cause death. If a potato is exposed to the sun, the concentration of this chemical will increase, particularly in the 'eyes' and under green patches. Such areas should be removed before cooking since they result in a bitter taste. It should be noted that solanine is destroyed in the cooking process and therefore does not present a health hazard in cooked potatoes.

Preparations
Note: continue until condition improves or as needed.

1. To treat ulcers, sour Stomach, intestinal infections, and constipation:
   - Wash, peel, and cut one fresh (unsprouted) potato. Grate, add small amount hot water to form a mash. Wrap the mash in a cloth, and squeeze the juice into a container. Take 1 or 2 tablespoons, sweetened with honey to taste, on an empty Stomach for 15 to 20 days. Avoid all spicy or sour foods. If effective, a person may continue treatment up to 30 days (use a fresh potato each day).

2. To treat skin eruptions and irritations, reddened blotches, scaling, itching, etc:
   - Repeat preparation in 1) above, apply the mash directly to skin irritation 4 - 6 times in 24 hours; wrap each application in a bandage. Repeat for 2 or 3 days.

3. For same conditions as 1) above (equally effective and more convenient):
   - Clean, peel, cut, and grate (in small amount hot water) 2kg of raw potatoes. Wrap the mash in a clean cloth and squeeze, collecting the juice. Pour the juice into a frying pan and cook over a low fire until it thickens into a paste. Add honey in an equal amount, mix and cook again until thick and sticky like putty. Let cool. Place in sealed container; keep in refrigerator. Eat 1-2 tablespoons, 1-2 times a day on an empty Stomach.

Method
Level II, Lesson 10

How to guide the swirl of Qi

Exercise objective: Learning to guide the swirl of Qi. The purpose of this exercise is to learn to turn the energy in the Dantien, to tonify the area associated with the Dantien and the organs contained in that area.

When is exercise performed: During normal Qigong practice, after moving the sun through the day and before the final meditation.

- Note: This is a three part Lesson taught over this Lesson and the next two.

1. Imagine a Tai Chi ball in the Dantien, a good image in this exercise is the image of the Yin/Yang symbol. Picture the two alternate colors in each spear as handles and then proceed to turn the handles in a circle thus moving the Qi ball around within the Dantien. Move in a clockwise direction. The center of the circle stays in one place and the Tai Chi ball turns around this " center."
   - Notes: (1) Some students find it helpful to picture a Tai Chi Sun. If this approach is helpful it should be used. (2) In doing this exercise the "clock" would be on the abdomen facing outward.
2. Swirl (circle) the Tai Chi ball 9 times in the Dantien, inhale up, exhale down.
3. This is one set, do 9 to 36 sets.
4. Begin meditation on the visualization of the Tai Chi ball or Tai Chi sun.

This Week's Sequence of Practice

1. Kidney Teeth Exercise
2. Wash
3. Deep Wash, Head, Shoulders, Hands
   Deep Wash, Back of Body
   Deep Wash, Front of Body
4. Gather the Yang/Hot Noon Sun
5. Gather the Yin/Earth's Negative Waters
6. Heart and Kidney in Harmony
7. Bring Heaven, Man and Earth Together for Harmony
8. Unite the Earth and Sky in the Body
9. Bring the Morning Sun
10. Expand and Contract the Sun
11. Move the Sun Through the Day
12. Swirl the Qi
13. Meditate
14. Quick or Full Close
15. Kidney Back Massage
16. Kidney Foot Massage

Student Journal

It is not necessary to travel the world to know its ways.
— Tao Teh Ching

Extra Thoughts – practice within your own limits

When practicing Qigong a person should not overextend the length of time they practice regardless of what type of Qigong is being done. There is a limit. If the length of time is extended tiredness may result. When a person thinks about practicing anything, the thought is often "the longer the better." This is not necessarily true. Consider the following ancient Chinese sayings:

"If you practice well (e.g. high level, very experienced), what you need will automatically be there."

And,

"If you want to reach the destination fast, you will not get there."

When a person practices Qigong they must be patient, relaxed, quiet, and natural. A person should be enduring and conscientious in advancing the study. Logic must be exercised in moving from easy to complicated (beginner to higher levels), from primary consideration and utilization of energy outside the body to deep within. The process cannot be rushed. If a person thinks that only one time or a short period of Qigong practice can cure a sickness, they are wrong and will be disappointed. In addition, this type of thinking can of itself create negative side effects. For example, if a person practices for too long a period of time, the person will become tired and energy will not be gained, rather it may actually be lost. In this situation the result would be that the sickness could become worse. Patience, trust in the method, and acceptance that the Qigong process will be different, but appropriate for each person, are principles which must be accepted.

Theory
Level II, Lesson 11

The basis of Chinese medical theory and its specialty.

The basis of the theory is its holistic perspective, harmonizing the body/mind with the individual's internal and external environment. In Chinese medicine the body and mind are perceived as a whole system. That system, in turn, has a specific relationship to its environment. The theory teaches that the body/mind must adapt to changes in the environment in order to remain in harmony (i.e., the body as microcosm within the macrocosm).

The specialty of Chinese medicine is in the theoretical perspective of its diagnosis and treatment of an illness, based on an understanding of the inter-relationships of internal organs connected through energy meridians. That is, symptoms (such as hair loss) are related to energy imbalances in certain principal organs (in this case, the Kidneys; similarly, diseases of the eye are related to the Liver). Thus, Chinese medicine treats body systems, rather than symptoms per se. This is in contrast to western medicine which addresses specific symptoms, most often manifested in a single body location.

Method
Level II, Lesson 11

How to guide the swirl of Qi

Exercise objective: Learning to guide the swirl of Qi. The purpose of this exercise is to learn to turn the energy in the Dantien and Mingmen, to tonify the areas associated with the Dantien and Mingmen and the organs contained in those areas.

When is exercise performed: In place of Level II, Lesson 10.

1. Imagine a Tai Chi ball in the Dantien..Turn the ball 9 times clockwise in the Dantien, then move the energy ball straight back through the body to the Mingmen.

2. Swirl (circle) the Tai Chi ball 9 times in a clockwise direction in the Mingmen. Then return the Tai Chi ball straight back through the body to the Dantien.
   - Note: the "clock" is on your back facing outward from the body when turning in the Mingmen.

3. This is one set, do 9 to 36 sets.

4. Begin meditation on the visualization of the Tai Chi ball or Tai Chi sun.

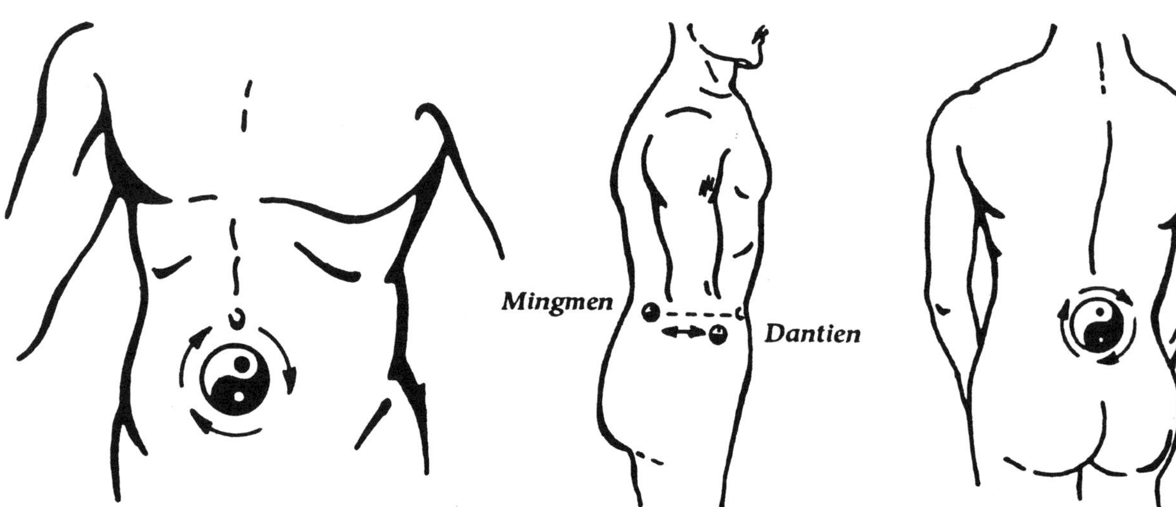

This Week's Sequence of Practice

1. Kidney Teeth Exercise
2. Wash
3. Deep Wash, Head, Shoulders, Hands
   Deep Wash, Back of Body
   Deep Wash, Front of Body
4. Gather the Yang/Hot Noon Sun
5. Gather the Yin/Earth's Negative Waters
6. Heart and Kidney in Harmony
7. Bring Heaven, Man and Earth Together for Harmony
8. Unite the Earth and Sky in the Body
9. Bring the Morning Sun
10. Expand and Contract the Sun
11. Move the Sun Through the Day
12. Swirl the Qi
13. Meditate
14. Quick or Full Close
15. Kidney Back Massage
16. Kidney Foot Massage

Student Journal

The Tao cannot be seen and has no name,
Yet leaves nothing undone.
— Tao Teh Ching

Extra Thoughts – organ theory

In TCM the internal organs of the body are basically divided into three groups; five viscera, six bowels, and extraordinary organs:

- Five viscera/zang/major — Liver, Heart, Spleen, Lung, Kidney, (plus the Pericardium)
  Major purpose: preserve vital substances

- Six bowels/fu/minor — Gall Bladder, Small Intestine, Stomach, Large Intestine, Bladder, Sanjiao (triple warmer)
  Major purpose: transmit and digest water and food

- Extraordinary — brain, medulla (marrow of the bones), bones, blood vessels, Gall Bladder, and the uterus
  Named separately because their functions are different

Organ theory directs its attention to the study of the physiological functions and pathological changes of every organ of the human body, and their interrelationships. Each organ has specific functions and relationships. A thorough knowledge of organ theory is required in order to understand what is occurring in the body in terms of balance/imbalance, its causes, and methods for correcting problems.

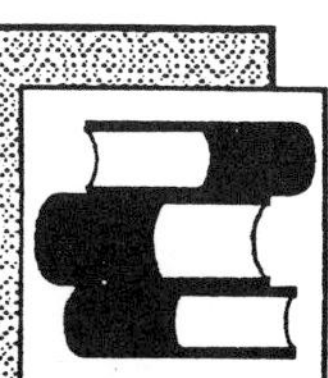

Eating and drinking to cure illness and prolong life – Part 9: ginger.

Energetic Nature of Food: The taste of ginger is pungent, its energy is strongly Yang, and it is non-toxic. It corrects a Yin imbalance and restores appetite.

Meridians: Ginger works through the Lung, Spleen, and Stomach meridians.

Explanation: Ginger is used as a daily spice in cooking. It is also effective as a health supplement. Use fresh ginger for cooking, aged ginger for health supplements.

Action: The action of ginger is to warm or heat the body, to open the pores and to cause perspiration. It acts as a diuretic, stops vomiting, and reduces inflammation in the Lungs.

Indications: Ginger is a good treatment for vomiting, for Yin Stomach gas, for inflammation of the Lungs, and for removing minor poisons in the system. It is also good for removing the odor of fish in cooking. Ginger peel is also effective in relieving water retention.

Contra-indications: Avoid ginger in the case of a Yang imbalance, excessive perspiration, and blood in the stool. Also avoid in case of a fever and/or Yang Stomach or Yang abdominal pain.

Preparations
Note: continue until condition improves or as needed.

1. To treat ulcers and vomiting (Yin Stomach):
   - Grate fresh ginger and squeeze the pulp, collecting 2 to 3 tablespoons of the juice. Mix with 1/2 bowl boiled water and drink to stop vomiting.

2. To treat food poisoning (spoiled meat or fish):
   - Boil 3 to 5 large slices fresh ginger in water (1 cup water, boil down to 1/2 cup); let cool and drink. Ginger can be eaten.

3) To treat hiccough:
   - Grate fresh ginger and squeeze the pulp for 2 to 3 tablespoons juice; mix with honey and drink.

4. To treat exposure to cold damp conditions (and diarrhea):
   - Mix 10g of ginger with equal amount of aged red tea leaves; boil 1-1/2 bowls water down to 1 bowl and drink. Discard tea leaves.

5) To treat abdominal pain:
   A. Chop 10 pieces ginger and white tips of 7 green onions; mash together to a paste. Add hot rice wine (1 to 2 tablespoons) and drink as internal medication.
   B. Prepare same mash mixture as indicated in (A) and place small amount in naval for 24 hours. Replace with fresh mixture. Continue until condition improves.

6. For menstrual blood loss, general aches and fever; to induce a sweat:
   - 15g ginger, 30g brown sugar; boil in water (start with 1-1/2 bowls and cook down to 1 bowl) and drink.

7. To treat excess gas in Stomach, intestines:
   - Pack a large whole piece of ginger root in yellow mud (clay), wrap in foil, and roast in oven until its aroma can be detected. (If clay is unavailable, just use foil.) Remove, clean, and slice. Place 1 large slice of ginger about the size of the thumb, in 1 cup boiling water, make an infusion, and eat and drink.

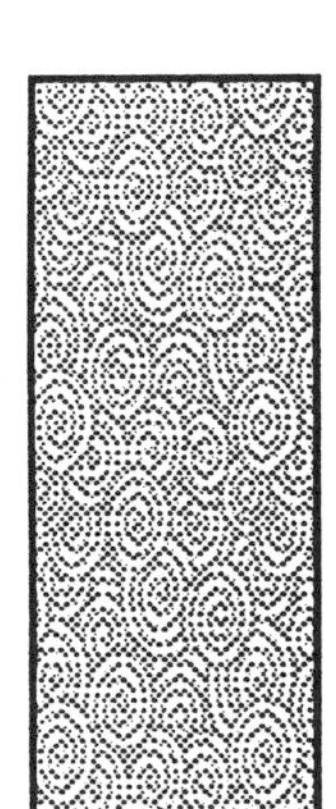

8. To treat frost bite:
   - Roast a whole piece of ginger root, slice, and rub gently on effected area.

9. To treat insect bites, bee stings and minor burns:
   - Grate ginger; place the mash directly on effected area.

10. To treat morning sickness and general nausea:
    - Mix 15g ginger with 10g dried orange peel; boil 1-1/2 cups water down to 1 cup and drink. You can eat or discard ginger and orange peel.

11. To treat falling hair, sporadic bald spots:
    - Cut ginger and apply exposed root directly to effected area.

Method
Level II, Lesson 12

How to guide the swirl of Qi

Exercise objective: Learning to guide the swirl of Qi. The purpose of this exercise is to learn to turn the energy in the Dantien and Mingmen, to tonify the areas associated with the Dantien and Mingmen and the organs contained in those areas.

When is exercise performed: In place of Level II, Lesson 10 and 11.

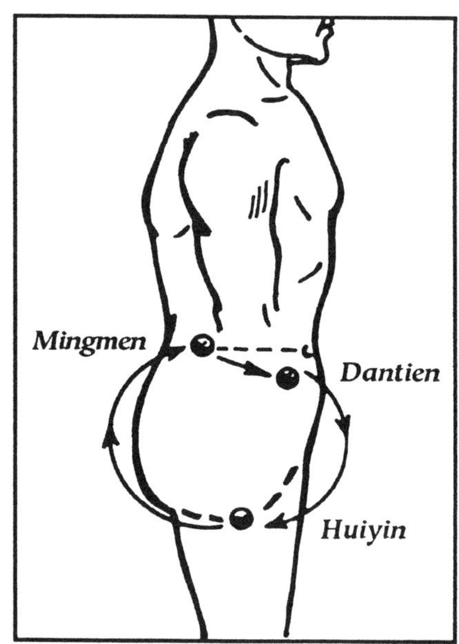

1. This exercise incorporates Lesson 10 and 11. The sun is in the Dantien. In the Dantien the sun is changed to the image of a Tai Chi ball. Then the Tai Chi ball is turned clockwise inside the Dantien 9 times.

2. Move the energy ball down to Huiyin (exhale) and then up to Mingmen (inhale). Rotate the energy ball clockwise in Mingmen 9 times in complete circles.

3. Inhale or exhale as you bring the energy ball straight through the body to Dantien.

4. Number 1, 2, and 3 above, combined, constitute one set. Do 3 to 36 sets.

5. Begin meditation on visualization of the Tai Chi ball or Tai Chi sun.
   - Note: This exercise is referred to as the "small-small circle."

This Week's Sequence of Practice

1. Kidney Teeth Exercise
2. Wash
3. Deep Wash, Head, Shoulders, Hands
   Deep Wash, Back of Body
   Deep Wash, Front of Body
4. Gather the Yang/Hot Noon Sun
5. Gather the Yin/Earth's Negative Waters
6. Heart and Kidney in Harmony
7. Bring Heaven, Man and Earth Together for Harmony
8. Unite the Earth and Sky in the Body
9. Bring the Morning Sun
10. Expand and Contract the Sun
11. Move the Sun Through the Day
12. Swirl the Qi
13. Meditate
14. Quick or Full Close
15. Kidney Back Massage
16. Kidney Foot Massage

Student Journal

When a learned person listens to the Tao,
They practice it tirelessly.
When an average person listens to the Tao,
They can't decide whether to believe it or not.
When an ignorant person listens to the Tao,
They laugh. But if such a person did not laugh,
The Tao would not be the Tao!
— Tao Teh Ching

Extra Thoughts – conclusion

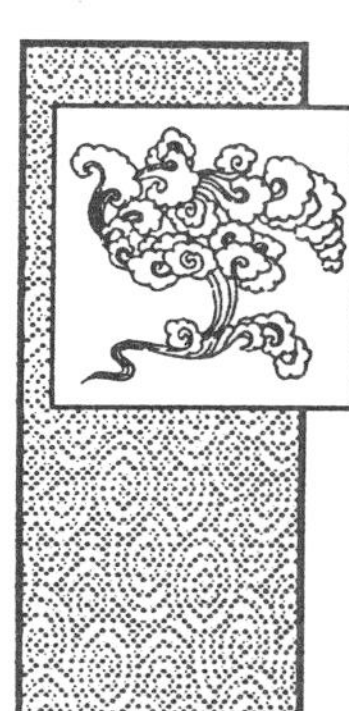

Qigong is an ancient discipline developed by the Chinese people. It was absorbed through experience, transforming work to relaxation, sickness to health, aging to longevity. Qigong is part of the Chinese medical tradition, along with herbology and acupuncture. It works on the balance of energy (Qi) in the body organs and meridians with a goal of maintaining a healthy body. The unique theory of Qigong is that it analyzes and explores the human body as a totality, rather than through the examination of individual parts or symptoms. The diagnosis and treatment of sickness and their prevention is thus considered in terms of the need for the creation (or recreation) of balance and harmony.

The theoretical basis for Qigong begins with the concept of Qi or energy. In practicing Qigong one develops "special" (cultivated) Qi to enhance the normal Qi which everyone possesses. This "special" Qi is collected and stored in the Dantien, which in turn strengthens the immune system and can be drawn on in case of illness or injury.

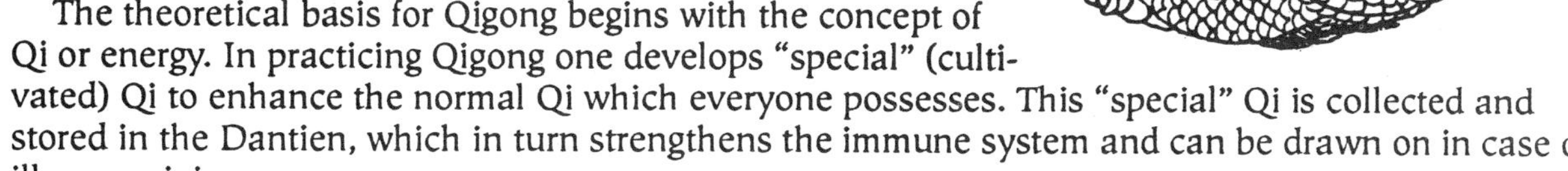

As the student progresses in Qigong study, the theoretical base expands to include an understanding of Yin/Yang theory; Five Element theory; Qi theory, Channel theory, etc. This includes a study of both internal and external factors and relationships; as well as food as a health supplement which, often in conjunction with herbs, can serve as a primary factor in the delicate balancing process required to maintain health, increase longevity, and as needed return the body from a state of imbalance (illness) to balance.

There are potential hazards to imbalance occurring and being allowed to remain untreated. Qigong helps prevent these hazards. For example:

- When one practices, "stuck" energy is released. This can prevent future problems caused by stagnation or blockages.
- Qigong teaches a person how to clear their emotions everyday, to release stress; this can help prevent illness because different emotions directly affect the organs.
- When a person has a serious organ problem, the problem most likely started a long time ago. It has been lying dormant, uncleared from the system. By studying Qigong we both release old problems and prevent problems from occurring in the future.

The importance of maintaining balance cannot be overemphasized.

Qigong is a system of exercises for fitness, but fitness as understood by Chinese medicine, which means fitness of the whole person; mind, body and spirit. Qigong is always a very personal and individual experience, however if desired, it can become a warm and rewarding group activity through sharing and the creation of relationships with fellow students. The potential rewards are many: relaxation, self-realization, exercise, meditation, self-healing, etc. In a society which seems to place most people in a constant race with their lives, Qigong can provide a much needed respite. Not dependent on age, previous experience, education, or physical prowess, it adjusts to each individual and allows them the flexibility to find a path suitable to their own physical and emotional needs.

As we move through our own personal life journey, we can not only help determine destinations, but we can make the journey more pleasant and healthier through the choices we make. One positive, ancient, yet modern choice can be to study and practice Qigong.

Having concluded the first two Levels of study of *Xuan Ming Dao* Qigong, you are on the path. I hope you will continue to learn and practice Qigong and that you will realize its many positive benefits.

— Student Reactions —

This section offers some examples of student reactions to the various exercises and the practice in general. It is not intended that all students should expect to have identical reactions. Every person reacts differently. However I felt you might find it interesting to know how others have responded to the exercises. Just by reading the diverse reactions noted, you can tell how many different types of experiences and benefits a single Qigong method can provide. These are some of the comments from my Xuan Ming Dao *Qigong students' evaluations and written comments when they were in Level I and II. These students were from all age ranges and a wide variety of backgrounds and physical conditions. I have included them because I think they accurately reflect, as a whole, student reactions. When students have expressed concerns in their comments, I have added an explanatory note.*

— Level I —

Washing/Cleansing

When I am stressed I think relax and go slowly. This exercise calms me down.

When my Heart is racing I use this exercise going slowly to return it to normal. Also works for anxiety feelings.

This one had such good imagery of the water surrounding the island — it was easy to remember.

Especially useful when stressed. It seems to clear the mind.

During the water cleansing little animals join me. They sit in groups and nibble the grasses.

I didn't realize that I was washing too much and sometimes I lost energy. The problem was corrected during a class discussion.

✵ *Note: It is important that a person not wash "too much." The general rule is not to wash over 6-9 times. Since most washes are releases, they can deplete the body, causing a feeling of emptiness, loss of energy, or tiredness. Also it should be remembered that after the wash is completed the student should always bring in a morning sun, meditate for at least a short time, and do the close. This insures that the "emptiness" created by the release is replaced with good energy.*

Cool and relaxed.

When pouring water into Baihui I feel a pressure between hands and top of head.

Helps relax — cleans thoughts and prepares body for the rest of practice.

Wonderful, downward rush.

Absorbing the positive forces from the sky (gathering Yang)

I can feel the heat moving down the center of my body. I can feel the Baihui open and the sun being pulled in.

This is like stoking a furnace. This really warms the body.

I feel warmth emanating from my hands, traveling down my arms into my chest and down to my Dantien.

I felt a lot of heat right away.

Very warm.

I feel a sort of waking up of the energy.

Connecting with the universal Yang.

Physically stretches my body.

Drawing in the earth's negative waters (gathering Yin)

About Level II I was able to clearly feel the difference between this earth/water/Yin energy and the hot Yang energy of the first exercise. It was really exciting. I began to understand what Sifu means when he says you must learn to distinguish the two types of energy if you want to be able to use them as needed.

When pouring the bowl into the Dantien I feel my Yongquan tingling.

Feeling grounded with new Yin practice. I felt my feet and legs more.

Legs feel very stimulated during this exercise.

A quieting effect.

Learned to adjust temperature of energy.

Physically the bending and weight shifting helped coordinate body.

Heart and Kidney in harmony (mixing fire and water)

Feels great, love the motion, leaves a feeling of balance and peace.

Easiest to do and to feel the Qi.

Twisting my back brings warmth to my Kidney area.

Very calming.

Feel very balanced after doing.

Smoothes and coordinates movement.

Bringing heaven, man, and earth together for harmony

At first this was hard because my legs hurt and this was distracting. But now I can feel my energy body stretch upward and bring the sky down. The mixing of the two in the Dantien feels good.

First time I felt energy body and control

Physically strengthening

Most powerful — I really like the way this feels.

When envisioning my energy body to grow I feel like I am touching the sky.

Uniting the earth and sky in the body

This exercise has been very difficult. I have trouble concentrating and connecting the energy.

- *Note: A person must practice this exercise for some time in order to be able to visualize, feel, and change the thought patterns, all at the same time.*

I become off balanced in this movement.

- *Note: Often if balance is difficult it indicates that the student is not keeping the Mingmen and Laogong connected or they are not maintaining the 70% concentration on the Mingmen.*

Feeling my hands get cool. As I rotate around I can feel my Dantien churn.

I have gained more flexibility in my spine from this exercise.

I felt pain in the Mingmen.

- *Note: Pain in points is most often a sign that the point is starting to open, or if there is a problem that the point is starting to release the problem. This is generally a good sign. Students should discuss issues related to pain with their teacher.*

It made me a little dizzy.

- *Note: Dizziness is often a sign that the 70% concentration on the Mingmen is not being kept or that the student is trying to turn too quickly. It is interesting because this same response can be experienced in the abdominal massage in the Complete Close if the person tries to circle that energy too quickly.*

Feel the earth and sky mixing and coming to Mingmen.

Physically increased flexibility.

Bringing the morning sun

I feel it coming in and going down.

If I don't concentrate I end up with no sun and I have to bring in the sun a second time!

When the sun reaches the level of my third eye (Tien Mu), it begins to feel like it is glowing.

- *Note: This is a good sign. The energy from Level I can open any point. However, in Level I in order to be safe, the student should not focus or concentrate on any area other than the appropriate thought pattern for the exercise being performed.*

Warming and centering.

Expand and contract the sun

For a long time it was difficult to feel the energy moving in all directions. At times I had to just concentrate on the back and the sides. The front was easier, I think this was because of the motion of the hands.

For a while I found my body swaying back and forth. Then the teacher explained that when we expand the sun it should expand not just to the front of us, but all around. As soon as I expanded the sun correctly my body stopped swaying. Dramatic proof to this skeptic that something is taking place.

My Dantien feels full when I do this.

Felt energy especially in the hands. There was a tingling and thickness in my hands.

I have an area on my right hip that holds stress and is painful. During one of the expand, contract breathing exercises I could feel the energy traveling to that area; then a great release there at the beginning of meditation.

✷ *Note: During the meditation concentration must be maintained on the Dantien. However if the Dantien becomes very "full," the energy may spill over on its own, and go to treat problem areas. If this occurs the student should allow it to happen, however the student must be certain that their focus remains on the Dantien.*

I have felt a letting go of some old emotional baggage. I also have a sense of well-being and a vast amount of energy available.

I stand up during the expansion and I love the wonderful connection of my body inner to outer during the expansion. I won't stop until the inner signals stop.

The "fire" and pain in my neck and shoulder has stopped.

Change for the better in grounding, breathing and pain control.

A painful hip problem has almost disappeared.

Very strong magnetic feeling, later able to adjust to heat, pressure, cold, etc.

Physically improved appetite, digestion and gave me a desire to eat more different types of food.

Meditation

My time in meditation varies more than I would like. Sometimes it is "perfect," relaxed, concentrated, etc., other times I really have to work at it.

If the exercises and visualization have gone well. If I have concentrated and not hurried, the meditation goes well. If I'm in a hurry and start to think of all the work I have to do, the meditation goes sour.

✷ *Note: It is important before you begin your practice that you try to clear the mind. Either resolve issues that are in your mind or troubling you, or consciously set them aside until after your practice. Simply say to yourself, "this is my time for Qigong practice and I will only focus on my pratice."*

In this Level (Level II), I felt a deeper spiritual connection in meditation versus a more noticeable physical connection in Level I.

I discover new levels of relaxation and concentration

Started with very rooted-centered feeling. Wonderful pictures and colors. Sometimes images of future events or regression.

During the meditation I have seen wonderful, interesting scenes. Sometimes its hard not to get involved and just let it happen.

I felt tingling in fingers and toes.

At first I had a hard time focusing and couldn't see colors.

✷ *Note: Students often experience difficulty in the beginning. By relaxing and not trying to force any experience, visualization, sensation, etc., to occur; and by continuing to practice regularly and well, that is follow the methods outlined; the student will progressively advance at the appropriate pace in the study.*

Quick close

I prefer this close to the complete close because the circular rubbing in the complete close makes me feel queasy.

✷ *Note: Normally if a person begins to feel upset to their stomach it means that they are turning the spiral too quickly.*

The quick close is just not enough.

Complete close

Wonderful sensations with the massage of face, ears, eyes, etc.

Feels great, activates and settles my whole body at the same time.

I had a hard time circling 36 times. I went past the area I was supposed to.

- *Note: It is very important to circle 36 times. In doing this part of the Complete Close many benefits are realized including: massage of the whole body; bringing the energy back and storing it; and, learning to control the energy. In addition the student must try to stay in the designated areas when doing this exercise.*

— *Level II* —

The basic fundamentals of Qigong-breath work — moving the sun through the day

The evening sun visualization bothers me. I do not like to think of myself standing in the water with the sun going down.

- *Note: This feeling may indicate a yang deficiency in the body. The student in this situation should discuss with the teacher the appropriate modification to the practice. Such a modification might be to make the water warmer and the sun warmer or hot.*

Re-enforces my connection to the environment.

Lots of things to change! However the protection really works well.

Have used this a lot for protection against people with problems, such as emotions (anger), or sickness (cold)

How the absorption of Qi massages the body/deep wash

I find this hard to get all the way through.

- *Note: Do not go quickly when doing this exercise, go more slowly. This reaction may mean that the body has a problem. It also may indicate that the student has not learned to be relaxed and patient in the practice.*

Great to do when upset. I've even done this when driving the car, getting stuck in traffic.

Wonderful, relaxing, refreshing.

Very cool and relaxing.

Helps me fall asleep.

Kidney back massage

All of the Kidney exercises have been very helpful.

Helps me wake up and also get extra energy.

A great refresher when I am tired.

Warms my back.

Kidney teeth exercise

Really don't like this one.

- *Note: Students need to understand the many benefits of this exercise. They should review the benefits listed in Method, Level II, Lesson 8.*

I hate doing it.

Relaxing, good prelude to practice.

Kidney foot/hand massage

I do the Kidney back and foot exercises when I'm tired or sore. It is very relaxing.

I do this in bed at night when I can't sleep. It is very effective for this purpose.

Helps remove soreness from whole legs.

Helped me when I had bad hot flashes.

How to guide the swirl of Qi

Helped to clear blockage in lower back.

Very hard for me to do. I have to concentrate so hard to get the Qi going in the right direction and then I have to keep count! This is not easy and I frequently fall asleep at this point.

✷ *Note: This may mean several different things. The person may not have enough energy. There may be a problem in the area. The person may not be very sensitive to energy yet, not uncommon in Level I and II. The last thing to remember is that this exercise may take some time to learn to do, patience is required and regular practice.*

Hard at first, but after practice it became easier.

Makes my head spin.

✷ *Note: The person must remember to maintain focus on the Dantien. Also it is important to try to remember to use the mind to do this, not the physical body. I have seen students who actually are turning their head around in circles trying to turn the circle, this can also lead to a feeling that the head is spinning. Remember that we are trying to connect the mind and the Qi as one aspect of this exercise.*

Really helped deepen the meditation.

General Reactions to the Practice

Helps clear and calm the mind, helps to collect myself after feeling pain.

I have a calmer feeling and it has reduced tension in my head. Made my breathing normal (an ongoing problem).

I feel very connected with the elements, sun sky, earth and water. Brought my energy to awareness.

Both the wash and moving the sun are helping me. I need to clean my body of toxins and tonify which is helping.

I feel more energy after doing the practice and also releases of blocked energy.

I feel great when I do it...calmer, peaceful, more focused and centered.

I noticed my health was good during PMS, my shoulder, which has been a problem, is much better.

Gets me nice and warm — Yea!

Calmer, less stressed.

Relaxed, alert, calm, centered.

I have chronic fatigue, with Qigong I am feeling a little better with more stamina, less mental grogginess.

Recently I had my first "normal" period in a long time, I am hoping this is a result of my Qigong practice.

Learning how to "wash" stuff out of me was great!

A sense of calm and well being. I feel lighter and more graceful. Much easier to fall asleep.

It seems like I have more energy for working out. I am stronger, my legs don't hurt as much. I am much more relaxed and positive.

I am very pleased about the quality of the instruction. Each class offers a very nice blend of theory, practice and philosophy. Sifu's approach is very integrated in that the student gets good insights into the whole approach. I feel I have made good progress in 12 weeks. After a two year search, I have found a teacher who can guide me on my path. I am looking forward to Level II.

It has been an extremely stressful period of my life. I feel that Tai Chi and Qigong practice have been very beneficial to me. I am much better able to handle stress. I look forward to class and practice.

Bringing energy and becoming more aware with increased energy. I also feel more balanced. It's better than a nap.

Sleeping better.

Can face the day more positively, more cheerful.

I felt calmer after someone's car accident.

Increased energy, better outlook on life.

Qigong is helping relieve the sadness of a lost one.

Evening practice is wonderful, I sleep well, wake up earlier than usual, more energy during the day.

This has made my yoga meditation more comfortable and longer.

I have not gotten sick and my pregnancy is going very well.

I feel the Qigong is really helping me in my life, physically, mentally, emotionally.

The Qigong helped my eye twitches. After six months I stopped feeling fluttering in my left eye. I experience more energy and less anxiety. My bunion problem has also improved.

I feel very calm and balanced, happy and warm.

My health is better. It's been positive. Bowel movement much more regular, more energy.

Better golf game, better concentration.

Energy work that is clearly in harmony with the present state of my life's evolution.

When feeling a bit negative or conflicted or burdened emotionally, the exercises bring me back into harmony.

More sensitive to foods. Tend to eat less prepared foods.

Sinuses are more open.

Made my body stronger against the winter.

My knee has improved

I used Qigong to eliminate a severe sore throat. Spending much time on cleansing and using the sun for destruction of negative cells.

I experienced physical exhaustion on Tuesday and did the entire practice flat on the floor in the morning. At the finish I felt very balanced and refreshed.

More in control of emotions.

I am becoming more introspective, for a greater part of my day. I find that I can be detached in chaotic situations where there may be too much emotionalism. I feel that I do have control over outer forces.

I have found this discipline to be totally different from anything I have ever practiced, really more personal and more self-involved.

Fibromyalgia in left shoulder blade seems to be improving.

A steady energetic pace during my workday. More awareness of what is going on in my body.

I feel calmer, stronger slightly. I had a decision to make which Qigong helped me make.

My chronic lower back pain improved and has not returned.

My tennis elbow, which is a chronic problem, seemed to "adjust" during two consecutive sessions, then stopped nagging.

I notice more things manifesting in the outer world, positive things.

Release of long held, chronic tension in right shoulder and right arm.

My health has been gradually improving.

My menopause problems have been greatly reduced.

I feel incredibly virtuous after practice.

I have generally more energy. Also, I have practiced a lot with moving energy into my feet to help reduce pain and I have much less pain.

Calmed knots in my stomach.

Seems that nerve pain in my leg has lessened.

It has helped relieve the insomnia. Also I am using ginger and potato recipes.

I have had a residual bronchitis. I feel much better the days I do my practice.

My back is easier to adjust for the chiropractor. Seems to be less pain.

I used to smile because we were instructed to do so. Now the smile is an automatic smile of pleasure during much of the practice.

In Level I and II I worked through two problems that I developed many years ago during two pregnancies. (A) In my second pregnancy I developed a condition of feeling dizzy if I stood in one place for any length of time, such as meeting and talking with people or standing in line at a store. I continued to have this condition for around 30 years. In the middle of Level I of Qigong, the condition completely disappeared. Now I can stand for any length of time and still feel comfortable. (B) In my first pregnancy I became sensitive to aromas, such as spices or fragrances. It made me feel nauseous. And this condition I also carried for around 30 years. In the middle of Level II Qigong, the condition disappeared. Now I can enjoy various aromas with no ill effects. I cannot pin-point the exact Lessons that caused the above "cures." I feel that all the cures I have experienced occurred synergistically through a series of Lessons.

Eased itching from poison ivy.

This style is much more balanced. The other Qigong I have learned was more Yang in nature and did not always provide opening and closing.

Soreness in finger joint is not as sore.

I feel like I am breathing a lot better.

Energy from Dantien healed completely a scalded arm in three days. A bad ear-ache was healed completely overnight.

In much of the practice I have made much progress in learning to follow directions. There has been some sort of block which is dissolving. I am feeling more confidence and my memory is better.

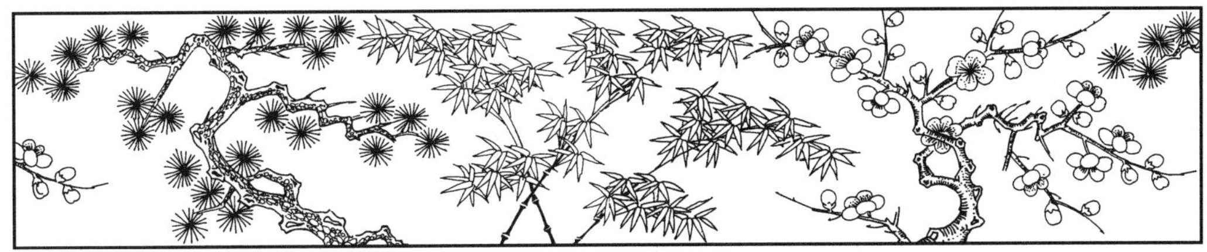

— About the Author —

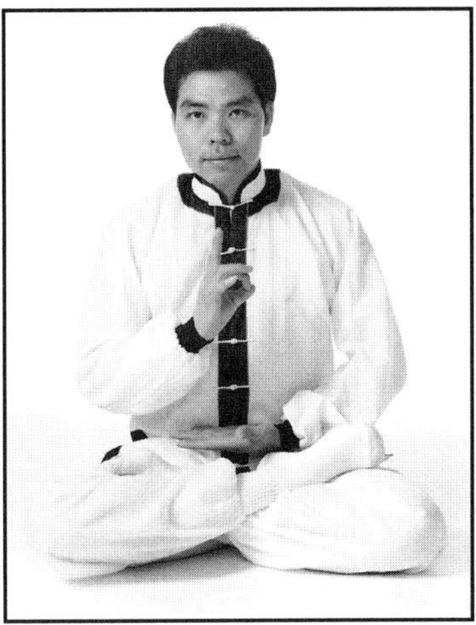

Master Huang has been in the United States since 1988. He has a background which combines aspects of both Chinese Healing and Chinese Martial Arts. He is a graduate of the *Guangzhou Traditional Chinese Medicine College* and a member of the *Guangdong Provincial Qigong Scientific Research Association* as well as a Qigong Advisor at the *South China Teaching University.* He is also a member of a number of professional organizations in his areas of expertise. Master Huang is a 31st generation disciple from the Shaolin Temple, he was South China Wushu Champion, and served as a National Judge of traditional Chinese Martial Arts in China. He is currently Master of the *Ching Ying Tai Chi Kung Fu Association* in Chicago. He is certified by the National Commission for the Certification of Acupuncturists (NCCA) in the United States.

Master Huang has presented a number of demonstrations and lectures in the Chicago area in both the field of Qigong and martial arts. He has also served as a judge of martial arts. One particularly significant demonstration occurred at the *Parliament of the World's Religions,* an international event held in Chicago in September of 1993.

Master Huang's English publications include a number of articles: "Preparing To Practice Qigong," *Qi Magazine* (Winter Issue, 1994); "Qigong, Chinese Wisdom for the 90s," *Enlightenments* (March, 1995); "How to Work With Disabled Students," *Tai Chi Magazine* (June, 1995); "Qigong, Handle With Care," *Qi Magazine* (Winter, 1996); as well as booklets on: *Traditional Chinese Healing* and *Self-Qigong, Acupressure and Massage*. In addition, *The Resource Guide,* and *The Chinese American News* have printed articles documenting Master Huang and his method of teaching Tai Chi and Qigong.

Master Huang currently teaches private and group lessons at a number of locations, conducts seminars, and offers counsel in the area of Traditional Chinese Healing.

To:

Yu-Cheng Huang
P.O. Box 166851
Chicago, IL 60616-6851

Please:

____ Add me to mailing list

____ Send information on classes, seminars and other materials available from the Ching Ying Tai Chi Kung Fu Association

____ Send information on tapes and videos

If a reply is requested, please include a self-addressed, stamped envelope.

Comments: *(remember to tell me how your practice is going)*

Name: ______________________________

Address: ______________________________

____

____

Phone: ______________________________

Tape or staple closed

Fold

From:

To:

Yu-Cheng Huang
P.O. Box 166851
Chicago, IL 60616-6851

Fold